MOSES

VOL. II

GOD STRENGTHENS HIS MAN

by Theodore H. Epp
Director
Back to the Bible Broadcast

A
BACK TO THE BIBLE
Publication

$1.50

Back to the Bible Broadcast

Box 82808   Lincoln, Nebraska 68501

100,000 printed to date—1975
(5-4423—100M—55)

Printed in the United States of America

Contents

Chapter   Page

1. God Strengthens His Man 5

2. Preparation for Israel's Exodus 9

3. The Progressive Strengthening 24

4. God's Strategy for Deliverance 44

5. The Progressive Hardening of Pharaoh's Heart . . 51

6. The Progressive Intensity of the Plagues . . . 68

7. The Progressive Compromises of Pharaoh . . . 90

8. The Final Judgment 107

Chapter 1

God Strengthens His Man

The emancipation of Israel from Egypt was in reality an intense conflict between two great personalities—God and Satan. Each person had prepared his man for this conflict.

Key Men—Moses and Pharaoh

For 80 years God had been preparing Moses to be His key person in this conflict. The time of preparation was so long because this was a gigantic task such as no other person had been called upon to do. Moses probably had a high IQ and many natural talents, as well as training in the courts of Egypt, but he had to have 40 years of special training alone with God in the desert. Those 40 years gave Moses his final preparation as God's man for emancipating Israel from Egypt.

But Satan also had his man—the God-defying Pharaoh. When Moses first appeared before him, Pharaoh said, "Who is the Lord, that I should obey his voice to let Israel go? I know not the Lord, neither will I let Israel go" (Ex. 5:2). Pharaoh's heart was hardened against God. God had forewarned Moses of this when He told him, "When thou goest to return into Egypt, see that thou do all those wonders before Pharaoh, which I have put in thine hand: but I will harden his heart, that he shall not let the people go" (4:21). However, God had also promised Moses, "I will stretch out my hand, and smite Egypt with all my wonders which I will do in the midst thereof: and after that he will let you go" (3:20). The subject of the hardening of Pharaoh's heart will be discussed in detail

5

later as we examine the plagues that God brought on Pharaoh and Egypt.

The conflict between God and Satan was really a one-sided conflict, for God had already told Moses, "Thou shalt say unto Pharaoh, Thus saith the Lord, Israel is my son, even my firstborn: and I say unto thee, Let my son go, that he may serve me: and if thou refuse to let him go, behold, I will slay thy son, even thy firstborn" (4:22,23). So these verses clearly indicate that the outcome of the conflict was already determined in the mind of God.

The Lord had told Moses, "Now shalt thou see what I will do to Pharaoh: for with a strong hand shall he let them go, and with a strong hand shall he drive them out of his land" (6:1). Even the Egyptians would know that Jehovah was God: "The Egyptians shall know that I am the Lord, when I stretch forth mine hand upon Egypt, and bring out the children of Israel from among them" (7:5).

Just as God and Satan conflicted concerning the emancipation of Israel from Egypt, so there will be conflict between them during a future time known as the Tribulation. This conflict is recorded in Revelation 4—20. Satan's man at that time will be the Antichrist, who will exalt himself as God.

Moses' Need for Strengthening

In considering the emancipation of Israel from Egypt, the early chapters of Exodus tell how God prepared His man for this task. Chapters 5—15 reveal how God strengthened His man. Moses needed to be strengthened so Pharaoh would realize that he was being confronted by God's man. Pharaoh needed to realize that he could not just ignore Moses because God was speaking through him.

Moses also needed to be strengthened because of his new position. He had been elevated from a shepherd, who was considered an abomination by the Egyptians, to God's personal spokesman against Pharaoh. Moses had to be strong as he was used by God in completely breaking the stubbornness of Pharaoh.

Pharaoh claimed to be a powerful god, but he soon discovered that he was no match for Moses and his God.

Later, God told Moses, "See, I have made thee a god to Pharaoh" (7:1). Although Pharaoh claimed to be a powerful god, he needed to realize that he was only a tool of God's enemy, Satan. When he refused the request to let Israel go, Moses replied that even the emperor of Egypt could not defy the God of Israel. It took a long time—possibly a year—before Pharaoh came to the same conclusion. God needed a strong man to make Pharaoh realize this, so it was necessary for Him to strengthen Moses for this great task.

As Moses came before Pharaoh to seek the emancipation of Israel, he conveyed more than a request of God that Pharaoh let the people go—it was a command. Since Pharaoh did not know God, he refused to recognize any power higher than himself. Moses assured him, however, that he would learn to know God in one way or another. Pharaoh chose the hard way. It took ten severe judgments, or plagues, to cause Pharaoh and his people to recognize the power of God and to understand that God meant what He said. The plagues continued until Pharaoh and his people were broken and destroyed, for they had set their wills against God. Pharaoh needed to know that God Almighty was undertaking the emancipation of Israel and that Moses was God's man of the hour. In studying the plagues that were brought on Pharaoh and the Egyptians, we will see that Pharaoh became progressively hardened against God while Moses became progressively stronger for God.

Israel's Preparation

On the other hand Israel, too, had to be prepared for the journey from Egypt to Canaan. In Genesis 15 the Israelites had been promised that after 400 years the nation would be brought out of captivity with a strong hand. This time element was completely fulfilled, so they needed to be prepared for the journey. At first they were unwilling because their faith in God was very weak. Although they had many problems in Egypt, they preferred to stay there rather than risk having nothing once they left.

There were two aspects to God's work in preparing the Israelites for what was ahead. First, three of the judgments, or plagues, were experienced by the Israelites as well as by the Egyptians. The Israelites experienced God's mercy and were spared from the last seven plagues. They saw the goodness of God in this, which led them to repent of their evil ways. Romans 2:4 states the scriptural principle: "The goodness of God leadeth thee to repentance."

Second, God also prepared Israel by revealing that Moses was His chosen leader. The Israelites had to be convinced that their deliverance was all God's undertaking, not their's. Little by little, God was able to teach them to rely on Moses as His representative. Moses himself became progressively bolder in his faith and more powerful in his leadership. One experience of faith led to another, just as one step leads to another. As Romans 1:17 says, "Therein is the righteousness of God revealed from faith to faith." The study of Moses' life and how he was strengthened by God is a study of how a believer progresses from faith to faith.

Chapter 2

Preparation for Israel's Exodus

As we study concerning the Israelites and what happened to them, let us remember the sobering words of I Corinthians 10:11: "Now these things happened to them as an example, and they were written for our instruction, upon whom the ends of the ages have come" (NASB). Thus, we need to carefully study what occurred during Old Testament times so that we can learn lessons for today.

Just as Moses needed to be prepared and strengthened by God for the task he was to accomplish we, too, need to be ready for what God wants us to do.

The Announcement to the Elders

When God first made it clear to Moses that he was the man He wanted to use to deliver Israel, Moses was reluctant because he was so sensitive about his deficiencies. Finally, however, Moses agreed to be God's representative, after he was convinced that the deliverance of Israel was to be God's work, not his. But because of Moses' insistence on his lack of eloquence, God permitted his brother Aaron to be his spokesman.

It was a memorable time when Moses and Aaron first announced to the Israelites that God was going to deliver them from Egypt. Exodus 4:29-31 records this significant time: "And Moses and Aaron went and gathered together all the elders of the children of Israel: and Aaron spake all the words which the Lord had spoken unto Moses, and did the signs in the sight of the people. And the people believed: and when they heard that the Lord had visited the children of

Israel, and that he had looked upon their affliction, then they bowed their heads and worshipped." Notice that Moses and Aaron presented their credentials. As the spokesman, Aaron "did the signs in the sight of the people." These signs were miracles that confirmed the fact that the message which Moses and Aaron delivered originated with God.

Moses must have been greatly encouraged by the response of the people, for they "bowed their heads and worshipped" (v. 31). Although this was a good response from the people, there were to be rough days ahead as the Israelites spoke out against Moses and his leadership.

But even though there were discouraging times later, the goodness of God allowed Moses and Aaron to see the favorable response of the people at this time. Although Moses and Aaron had confidence in God, their faith was rather weak, so this initial response of the people was highly significant. They saw God's ability to work in the lives of the Israelites and were tremendously encouraged. A rebuff at this point might have been a tragedy in Moses' life.

God did not test Moses beyond what he was able to endure. The New Testament tells of God's goodness in regard to this matter: "No temptation has overtaken you but such as is common to man; and God is faithful, who will not allow you to be tempted beyond what you are able; but with the temptation will provide the way of escape also, that you may be able to endure it" (I Cor. 10:13, NASB). When God allows a temptation, or testing, He also makes available sufficient grace for the Christian to be able to stand in spite of it. He does not allow the believer to be tested beyond what he is able to bear. The trial of our faith is very important, but only God knows how much trial we can take at any one time. And because of His faithfulness and goodness, He does not push the believer beyond his limit.

First Meeting With Pharaoh

Having had their first meeting with the elders of Israel, Moses and Aaron then had their first meeting with Pharaoh. God had already told Moses that Pharaoh would not listen to him, but He made it clear to Moses that by the time God was through with Pharaoh, he would listen. Although God had told Moses about the eventual slaying of the firstborn if Pharaoh did not let the Israelites go, Moses and Aaron did not mention this to Pharaoh when they first appeared before him. They simply announced to Pharaoh, "Thus saith the Lord God of Israel, Let my people go, that they may hold a feast unto me in the wilderness" (Ex. 5:1).

Pharaoh was far from being impressed by Moses and Aaron or by the God of Israel. Pharaoh said, "Who is the Lord, that I should obey his voice to let Israel go? I know not the Lord, neither will I let Israel go" (v. 2).

Had Moses and Aaron immediately told Pharaoh that the firstborn of Egypt would be killed if he did not let Israel go, the hardness of Pharaoh's heart might not have been demonstrated. But even this simple request which they made of him caused the hardness of Pharaoh's heart to become immediately apparent. Pharaoh was considered a god, and, as such, worship was directed to him. God would eventually break him of his haughtiness, but first He was going to reveal to Israel, to Moses and Aaron and to us today that Pharaoh was a hardened individual to begin with. Pharaoh failed to recognize that God puts on the throne whomever He wills, and He removes from the throne whomever He wills. God could have immediately taken care of Pharaoh, but He did not do so, for there were many lessons to be taught through the hardness of this individual.

The key to understanding all that was involved is Exodus 5:2, which records Pharaoh's refusal to recognize anyone higher than himself. He was considered a god, and he was not about to let any other being receive greater recognition than himself. In essence, he told Moses and Aaron, "I do not recognize your God. I will not obey Him. No one is going to tell me what I can or cannot do!"

Pharaoh thus hardened his own heart against God Almighty. Concerning Pharaoh the New Testament says, "For the scripture saith unto Pharaoh, Even for this same purpose have I raised thee up, that I might shew my power in thee, and that my name might be declared throughout all the earth" (Rom. 9:17). Verse 22 adds, "What if God, willing to shew his wrath, and to make his power known, endured with much longsuffering the vessels of wrath fitted to destruction." Inasmuch as Pharaoh hardened his own heart against God, he became one of the "vessels of wrath fitted to destruction."

God did not make Pharaoh a vessel fit for destruction; Pharaoh did that himself. God had much longsuffering, or patience, with him. God only added to the hardening process already evident in Pharaoh's life.

We sometimes say that, because of His foreknowledge, God knew that all of this was going to take place. However, it is not as if God sees things as future. Since God knows everything, it is as if everything were in the present tense to Him. We think of events as being past, present or future, but the whole future is before God just as though it were present. In other words, everything to God is in what I like to call the "ever-present tense." We are creatures of time, but He works with everything in constant view before Him. That is why Romans 8:28 is such a precious verse: "All things work together for good to them that love God, to them who are the called according to his purpose." God knows what is ahead, so He can cause all things to work together for our good.

Pharaoh's rejection of God's command to let Israel go was allowed by God for several other reasons. First, Pharaoh's behavior was tolerated so the world would know that the God of heaven has thoroughly subdued everything that is called god. Second, it was allowed so that Israel might be brought to a singular knowledge of God. The nation was in a backslidden condition and needed a greater respect of God's hatred of sin. Third, Pharaoh's rejection of God's authority made Israel willing to leave Egypt. Even though they were oppressed by the Egyptians, they were not ready and willing to leave. Thus, God had to make them willing (see Phil. 2:13). Fourth, Moses and Aaron needed to realize that the task of delivering Israel was hopeless if they relied on their own strength. Only the God of heaven could cause Pharaoh to change his mind. Fifth, the Israelites needed a greater concept of who God is and what He wanted to do for them. Their estimate of God was far too low. They needed to learn the truth that "God is our refuge and strength, a very present help in trouble" (Ps. 46:1).

God's Mercy and God's Judgment

The nation of Israel realized that it did not have answers to the problems it faced. Most nations today also recognize the same thing. They have many overwhelming problems which they do not know how to cope with—population explosions, inflation, famine. The tendency is for one nation to rise up against another nation in an attempt to satisfy its needs and solve its problems. The Scriptures indicate that world conditions are going to get much worse before they get better. In fact, we will not really have world peace until the Prince of Peace comes to establish His kingdom on earth. When Christ comes to set up His earthly kingdom, He will first bring judgment on the nations. But as is customary in God's manner of working, grace is always abundantly manifested before judgment.

Although a day of judgment is coming, as described in the Book of the Revelation, God is abundantly extending His mercy at the present time. Just as God gave 120 years of mercy before the judgment of the flood in Noah's time, so now the nations are being given a chance to repent and return to God as the preaching of the gospel is heard in all parts of the world. Never in the history of the world has there been a time when the gospel has been preached as much and as clearly as it is today—from one end of the world to the other. This is being accomplished through a variety of means such as missionaries, radio, literature and Bible translators.

But we must remember that God's salvation is more than just an invitation to get right with God. God's plan of salvation involves a declaration of what God demands of the sinner. Of course, He demands it in love, but it is still a demand. Just as God was demanding Pharaoh to let His people go, so God demands certain things of us. Acts 17:30 says that God "commandeth all men every where to repent." This is not an option; if we are to be right with God, we must repent. The word "repent" includes more than sorrow; it is actually a change of mind. No one can come into right relationship with God until he changes his mind about who God is, about his sin and about the need to have that sin taken care of. Those who never change their minds about these things never come to God trusting in Jesus Christ alone for salvation.

Having trusted Jesus Christ as Saviour, the believer's life will be drastically different. This is especially true as he looks forward to the coming of Christ. Concerning the return of Christ, I John 3:3 says, "And every man that hath this hope in him purifieth himself, even as he is pure." What a wonderful hope the believer has once he has placed his trust in Jesus Christ!

But how sad it will be for those who continue to reject Christ as Saviour. Second Thessalonians 1:8 refers to those unsaved who will be living at the time of Christ's return to earth: "In flaming fire taking vengeance on them that know not God, and that obey not the gospel of our Lord Jesus Christ." The following verse reveals the awful judgment that these people will experience: "Who shall be punished with everlasting destruction from the presence of the Lord, and from the glory of his power" (v. 9). If the gospel is not obeyed, judgment is sure. The more light that is given and rejected, the more terrible will be the judgment on the unbeliever.

To turn away from the light and the truth of God causes one to become more and more hardened in sin. Whereas the manifestation of the grace and mercy of God causes some to respond to Him, it seems to cause others to rebel all the more. The same sun that melts the ice hardens the clay. And often, the sun of God's mercy and grace melts some hearts but hardens others.

Pharaoh was one who turned his face against Almighty God and continued to reject Him. Any manifestation of the grace of God only served to harden Pharaoh's heart all the more until he was one of "the vessels of wrath fitted to destruction" (Rom. 9:22).

Background for God's Action

The fifth and sixth chapters of Exodus provide the background for all that followed. Exodus 5:9 reveals how lightly Pharaoh thought of the words of God. As Pharaoh instructed his men to make the Israelites' work load heavier, he said of the Israelites, "Let them not regard vain words." Pharaoh was referring to the words spoken to him by Moses and Aaron, which were the words of God. Pharaoh considered the mandate given to him by God through Moses as "vain words." No one can think this lightly of the words of God and escape judgment.

So God worked with Pharaoh not only to reveal that he was a vessel "fitted to destruction" but also to make Israel willing to leave the land of Egypt. When Moses and Aaron first met with the elders of Israel, they gladly accepted God's promise of deliverance, and "they bowed their heads and worshipped" (4:31). But later it was evident that the Israelites were not really willing to leave Egypt. Thus, even Pharaoh's response and his act of increasing the work load of the Israelites were used by God to make the Israelites willing to leave Egypt.

The foremen of the Israelites were so upset with the increased work load that they bypassed Moses and went directly to Pharaoh. When Pharaoh refused to lighten their work load, the foremen lashed out at Moses and said, "The Lord look upon you, and judge; because ye have made our savour to be abhorred in the eyes of Pharaoh, and in the eyes of his servants, to put a sword in their hand to slay us" (5:21). The people were far from ready at that time to forsake Egypt for the uncertainty of the desert trip ahead of them. So God was preparing them in a special way, even though they could not understand it at the time. God was allowing them to experience grief so He could bring about His will in their lives. This reminds us of Lamentations 3:32: "But though he cause grief, yet will he have compassion according to the multitude of his mercies." Although God may allow believers to experience grief for a time, it is for the purpose of later showing His mercy.

After Moses had been rejected by Pharaoh and by his own people, he was left alone with God. "Moses returned unto the Lord, and said, Lord, wherefore hast thou so evil entreated this people? Why is it that thou hast sent me? For since I came to Pharaoh to speak in thy name, he hath done evil to this people; neither hast thou delivered thy people at all" (Ex. 5:22,23). Moses was completely at the end of himself; he had nowhere to turn but to God. This set the stage for all that followed. Pharaoh defied God; Israel rejected God's plan and saw no hope; Moses saw himself as helpless and cast himself on God alone. Then God was ready to act.

God's Promise

This significant statement follows: "Then the Lord said unto Moses, Now shalt thou see what I will do to Pharaoh: for with a strong hand shall he let them go, and with a strong hand shall he drive them out of his land" (Ex. 6:1).

Although these words of God to Moses sounded as if they might be fulfilled the next day, it was actually several months, maybe even a year, before they were fulfilled. Several steps were involved in the process, and Moses had to learn to wait on God.

One of the key words in this verse is "now." God was, in effect, telling Moses, "Now that you are where you ought to be, Moses, I will begin to act." Israel had been crushed under Pharaoh's inhuman work assignments, and Pharaoh had essentially challenged God to a duel.

Another key word is "I"—"what I [God] will do." Since Moses had learned that he was not to rely on anyone except God Himself, God promised that Moses would see what He would do to Pharaoh. And when God was finished with Pharaoh, He would show Moses what He was going to do with Israel. Moses' responsibility was to simply rest on the promises of God. During his 80 years of preparation, Moses had learned to know God.

The words of Exodus 6:1 amounted to God giving His final word to Moses. The word of God is just as reliable as God is. Because God has complete integrity, He always honors His word. Isaiah 55:11 records this promise of God: "So shall my word be that goeth forth out of my mouth: it shall not return unto me void, but it shall accomplish that which I please, and it shall prosper in the thing whereto I sent it."

Exodus 6 emphasizes the importance of the name of God. God told Moses, "I am the Lord: and I appeared unto Abraham, unto Isaac, and unto Jacob, by the name of God Almighty, but by my name Jehovah was I not known to them" (vv. 2,3); "Wherefore say unto the children of Israel, I am the Lord" (v. 6).

The words "I am the Lord," appearing in verses 2 and 6, serve as brackets for all that is in between. What is said between these statements pledges the very nature of God Himself to accomplish what is promised. What God promised is indicated by seven "I wills" in verses 6-8. "I will bring you out from under the burdens of the Egyptians" (v. 6); "I will rid you out of their bondage" (v. 6); "I will redeem you with a stretched out arm" (v. 6); "I will take you to me for a people" (v. 7); "I will be to you a God" (v. 7); "I will bring you in unto the land" (v. 8); "I will give it you for an heritage" (v. 8).

The words that serve as brackets, "I am the Lord," clinch the promises of God. He had revealed Himself to Moses as "I Am That I Am" (3:14). All that Moses needed, God would be to him, and this was what God emphasized in His promises recorded in Exodus 6. Whatever was needed to fulfill the promises, God was more than able to supply. This was true concerning Israel, and it is also true concerning us. Whatever our need is, He is able to meet it.

In analyzing the "I wills" in Exodus 6:6-8, it is possible to group them into three categories. The first three, which appear in verse 6, have to do with emancipation. The Lord said, "I will bring you out from under the burdens of the Egyptians, and I will rid you out of their bondage, and I will redeem you with a stretched out arm, and with great judgments."

The next two "I wills," which appear in verse 7, have to do with God's taking the nation of Israel to Himself. He said, "I will take you to me for a people, and I will be to you a God: and ye shall know that I am the Lord your God, which bringeth you out from under the burdens of the Egyptians."

The last two statements, which appear in verse 8, have to do with assurance of victory in the spiritual warfare that Israel faced. God said, "I will bring you in unto the land, concerning the which I did swear to give it to Abraham, to Isaac, and to Jacob; and I will give it you for an heritage: I am the Lord."

Reactions of Israel and Pharaoh

These promises of God were delivered by Moses to the Israelites, but they rejected his message. The Bible says,

"Moses spake so unto the children of Israel: but they hearkened not unto Moses for anguish of spirit, and for cruel bondage" (v. 9). It is important to remember, however, that Moses discharged his responsibility by passing on God's message to the people. What they did with the message was their responsibility. So, too, in witnessing our responsibility is to give others the message of salvation; how they respond to it is their responsibility. So we need not answer the question, How many have responded to the message? The question we must answer is, Have I been faithful to my responsibility in giving out the message?

During his years of walking with the Lord, Moses had learned that he was not responsible for the reactions of others. He had learned that his responsibility was to discern God's message and to faithfully deliver it to others. The Lord had promised to bring the nation of Israel out of Egypt, but in order for an individual to participate in the fulfillment of that promise, he had to respond by faith. Studying how God took care of Israel in the wilderness proves that God was faithful to every promise He had made to them.

Although the Israelites rejected Moses' message, God instructed Moses to go before Pharaoh once again. God told Moses, "Go in, speak unto Pharaoh king of Egypt, that he let the children of Israel go out of his land" (v. 11). But Moses had problems with this commission of God. Since the Israelites had not accepted his message, what was the use of going before Pharaoh? Moses told God, "Behold, the children of Israel have not hearkened unto me; how then shall Pharaoh hear me, who am of uncircumcised lips?" (v. 12). But, in effect, God told Moses, "You leave Pharaoh to me. Remember, I told you that you would see what I was going to do with Pharaoh."

Then, the Bible records, "The Lord spake unto Moses and unto Aaron, and gave them a charge unto the children of Israel, and unto Pharaoh king of Egypt, to bring the children of Israel out of the land of Egypt" (v. 13).

Pharaoh disregarded any other god speaking to him; he made that very clear (see 5:2). Pharaoh was not going to have anyone telling him what to do—not even God!

But Pharaoh was in for a surprise! God told Moses, "See, I have made thee a god to Pharaoh: and Aaron thy brother shall be thy prophet" (7:1). Before God was through dealing with Pharaoh, Pharaoh would recognize Moses' power over him, because Moses was God's representative. Moses had authority because he spoke for God and with God's authority.

In the New Testament the authority of God is seen in the words of Christ: "All power [authority] is given unto me in heaven and in earth" (Matt. 28:18). In the same passage the Lord promised believers: "I am with you alway, even unto the end of the world [age]" (v. 20).

Exodus 7:1 indicates that Aaron was to be Moses' prophet; that is, he was to be Moses' mouthpiece. So as far as Pharaoh was concerned, Moses would be in the place of God over him, and Aaron would be Moses' prophet, or spokesman.

As a god over Pharaoh, Moses would rule Egypt in that he would have Egypt under his domination as he controlled Pharaoh. Moses was to tell Pharaoh what he must do, what he should expect to happen, and that he must appeal to Moses for relief from the plagues. As we study the plagues later, we will see how God made Moses a god to Pharaoh.

God told Moses, "Thou shalt speak all that I command thee: and Aaron thy brother shall speak unto Pharaoh, that he send the children of Israel out of his land" (v. 2). The words were not to be of Moses' choosing—he was to speak what God told him to speak.

We, too, are to be faithful in delivering God's message to an unbelieving world. Through the Apostle Paul God commands us, "Preach the word; be instant in season, out of season" (II Tim. 4:2). The reason for the urgency is stated in verse 3: "For the time will come when they will not endure sound doctrine." No wonder Paul told Timothy earlier in the same epistle to "hold fast the form of sound words, which thou hast heard of me" (1:13). It is a principle with God that when He gives a charge, He also gives the power to accomplish it. So we may be sure that when we act on His Word, the power to perform the task will be provided.

God told Moses, "I will harden Pharaoh's heart, and multiply my signs and my wonders in the land of Egypt" (Ex. 7:3). Although God announced that He would harden Pharaoh's heart, He did not say when He would do it. It

seems, however, from the context that God did not harden
Pharaoh's heart until the latter part of Moses' dealing with
him. It is not until Exodus 9:12 that we read: "The Lord
hardened the heart of Pharaoh," and this was after the sixth
plague. Until that time God exercised His mercy and gave
Pharaoh every opportunity to turn to Him.

The Contest

The total commitment of Moses and Aaron to God's will
is seen in Exodus 7:6: "And Moses and Aaron did as the
Lord commanded them, so did they." They did exactly as
God said. So the contest began in earnest.

Although it appeared to be Moses and Aaron against
Pharaoh, it was really God against Satan. Because of the
omnipotence of God, the outcome of the contest was never
in question. From the human viewpoint, however, it was a
real contest, and people had to decide whether they would be
on the side of God or Satan. All that God asked of His
servants was absolute obedience so He could work through
them to accomplish His will.

In total obedience to God's command, Moses and Aaron
went before Pharaoh. The Bible says, "They did so as the
Lord had commanded: and Aaron cast down his rod before
Pharaoh, and before his servants, and it became a serpent"
(v. 10). For Moses and Aaron this amounted to the
presentation of their credentials. They represented a
miracle-working God, and they had come to speak in His
behalf.

But notice what Pharaoh did—he called the "wise men
and the sorcerers: now the magicians of Egypt, they also did
in like manner with their enchantments. For they cast down
every man his rod, and they became serpents" (vv. 11,12).

The ability of the magicians of Egypt to imitate the
miracles of Moses and Aaron should teach us many important
lessons. One crucial lesson that we especially need to learn
today is that everything supernatural is not necessarily of
God. Today, experience and unusual happenings are
emphasized, but it takes much wisdom to know whether or
not the unusual is really of God.

In referring to the contest between Pharaoh's magicians and Moses and Aaron, the Apostle Paul said, "Now as Jannes and Jambres withstood Moses, so do these also resist the truth: men of corrupt minds, reprobate concerning the faith" (II Tim. 3:8). These two names, "Jannes" and "Jambres," were apparently part of Jewish tradition that had been handed down since the time of Pharaoh. As Paul wrote, the Holy Spirit superintended so he did not select erroneous details from Jewish tradition. In selecting these names, Paul identified the two men who exercised leadership among the magicians of Egypt in opposing Moses and Aaron. Notice what Jannes and Jambres had in common with the false teachers of Paul's day: "Men of corrupt minds, reprobate concerning the faith" (v. 8).

The Power of Satan

Even though the magicians of Egypt were able to perform some miracles, there were many miracles they could not perform. But let us not miss the point that there were *some* they were able to perform. No doubt they were able to do these by the power of Satan, who energized them.

During the coming Tribulation Satan's man will be the Antichrist. The Antichrist will be the prominent personality during the seven-year Tribulation, and he will exercise control over the entire world. A person known as the "false prophet" will direct worship to the Antichrist. In referring to the false prophet, Revelation 13:13-15 says, "He doeth great wonders, so that he maketh fire come down from heaven on the earth in the sight of men, and deceiveth them that dwell on the earth by the means of those miracles which he had power to do in the sight of the beast; saying to them that dwell on the earth, that they should make an image to the beast, which had the wound by a sword, and did live. And he had power to give life unto the image of the beast, that the image of the beast should both speak, and cause that as many as would not worship the image of the beast should be killed." Thus, we see how Satan will deceive the world through miracles.

Referring to the Antichrist, II Thessalonians 2:9,10 says, "Even him, whose coming is after the working of Satan with all power and signs and lying wonders, and with all deceivableness of unrighteousness in them that perish; because they received not the love of the truth, that they might be saved."

From the Book of Job we also see that Satan has definite powers. Satan came before the presence of God and challenged Him concerning Job. Satan told God that the only reason Job was serving Him was that God had given him so much. Satan asked, "Does Job fear God for nothing? Hast Thou not made a hedge about him and his house and all that he has, on every side? Thou hast blest the work of his hands, and his possessions have increased in the land. But put forth Thy hand now and touch all that he has; he will surely curse Thee to Thy face" (Job 1:9-11, NASB).

At that point God allowed Satan to take away what Job had, but God did not allow him to touch Job himself. God said, "All that he hath is in thy power; only upon himself put not forth thine hand" (v. 12). First, Job's oxen and donkeys were stolen and his servants killed by the attacking Sabeans (vv. 14,15). Then fire fell from heaven and burned up his sheep and the servants that were with them (v. 16). Next, the Chaldeans attacked and stole his camels and killed the servants who were tending them (v. 17). But the worst of all was the great wind which struck the house where his sons and daughters were gathered, killing them all (vv. 18,19).

These incidents demonstrate the power that Satan was able to exercise as God permitted him to do so. But Job still did not curse God as Satan thought he would, so Satan challenged God to let him touch Job's body. God also permitted this, and the Book of Job is an account of how God proved His ability to hold on to Job even in the midst of Job's intense suffering.

The Power of God

Just as God allowed Satan to go only so far in attacking Job, so He allowed the magicians of Egypt to go only so far and no further. Notice what happened when their rods became serpents: "Aaron's rod swallowed up their rods" (Ex. 7:12). That which makes this entire incident so significant is the fact that the serpent was worshiped in Egypt. It was considered a god, and the fact that Aaron's rod consumed the rods of the Egyptians revealed that God was pronouncing doom on the lying wonders and the serpent gods of Egypt. In addition to teaching the lesson God intended for the Egyptians, this act was no doubt of great encouragement to Moses and Aaron as they realized that God was working through them to perform miracles in order to accomplish His will. This was a fulfillment of God's promise that they would have power over the Egyptians and, in particular, that Moses would be made a "god to Pharaoh" (v. 1). In this first real encounter, it was evident that the gods of Egypt could not stand before the God of Moses and Aaron.

Chapter 3

The Progressive Strengthening

In considering how God strengthened Moses, we learn that Moses progressed in faith, boldness and power with both God and man.

It is important to reflect on how God had already worked with Moses before considering how God strengthened him further. After spending 40 years in God's special school in the wilderness, Moses was told, "Go, return into Egypt: for all the men are dead which sought thy life. And Moses took his wife and his sons, and set them upon an ass, and he returned to the land of Egypt: and Moses took the rod of God in his hand" (Ex. 4:19,20). Notice that he took with him the shepherd's rod, which would always remind him of his nothingness and of the need to depend entirely on God.

Going Backward With God

At that time God warned Moses that Pharaoh would refuse to let the Israelites go. The Lord told Moses, "When you return into Egypt, see that you do before Pharaoh all those miracles and wonders which I have put in your hand; but I will make him stubborn and harden his heart, so that he will not let the people go" (v. 21, Amplified). In a sense, this warning that Pharaoh would reject his plea let Moses know that he had to experience defeat before he could experience victory. Moses had to know what it was to go backward before he could go forward!

I will never forget an incident that taught me this lesson in relation to Back to the Bible in the early 1940s. I had invited a minister to preach a series of evangelistic messages on the radio, and during that time we were having some extremely difficult financial struggles. Things certainly looked as if they were going backward. One day he and I met to pray especially about these matters. Before we prayed, he made this significant statement: "Brother Epp, it takes more faith to go backward with God than to go forward with God." I have never forgotten that statement!

It was necessary for Moses to be so committed to God that he could go backward with Him before going forward. Moses needed to have an unshakable faith in God, and this is what he acquired during the 40 years in the desert alone with God.

As Moses experienced the expected refusal of Pharaoh and the unexpected reaction of his own people, he saw that he was not to put trust in man but only in God. This was the key to Moses' future success. Had he not learned this lesson, God could not have used him as He later did.

As Moses experienced these setbacks, he actually went forward in his confidence in God. He had to learn the same lesson that the nation of Israel learned later when its armies were endangered. Hezekiah told the people, "Be strong and courageous, be not afraid nor dismayed for the king of Assyria, nor for all the multitude that is with him: for there be more with us than with him" (II Chron. 32:7). The Israelite army was smaller than the Assyrian army, but the significant difference was not in size but in the one in whom they were trusting. Referring to the king of Assyria, Hezekiah said, "With him is an arm of flesh; but with us is the Lord our God to help us, and to fight our battles" (v. 8).

Jeremiah warned against trusting in the arm of flesh when he said, "Thus saith the Lord; Cursed be the man that trusteth in man, and maketh flesh his arm, and whose heart departeth from the Lord. Blessed is the man that trusteth in the Lord, and whose hope the Lord is" (Jer. 17:5,7). We need to learn this lesson also. We must not put our confidence in people—good as they may be. This does not mean that we should not trust others, but it means that in the final analysis our confidence must be in God alone. We should never think when we encounter a problem that it can be automatically solved just by getting enough people to help with it. The Bible tells us: "Trust in the Lord with all thine heart; and lean not unto thine own understanding. In all thy ways acknowledge him, and he shall direct thy paths" (Prov. 3:5,6).

It was a horrible expression of ingratitude on the part of Israel for them to turn against Moses after Pharaoh had made their work load heavier. They told Moses, "The Lord look upon you, and judge; because ye have made our savour to be abhorred in the eyes of Pharaoh" (Ex. 5:21). But this, as well as Pharaoh's rejection, drove Moses to depend on the Lord alone. Verse 22 says, "Moses returned unto the Lord." I love that statement—Moses had nowhere else to turn, so he was forced to turn to the Lord.

The experiences Moses had at this time enabled him to take a firm stand for the Lord later when Israel was before the Red Sea with seemingly no way of crossing or escaping from the pursuing Egyptians. Moses courageously told the people, "Fear ye not, stand still, and see the salvation of the Lord, which he will shew to you to day: for the Egyptians whom ye have seen to day, ye shall see them again no more for ever. The Lord shall fight for you, and ye shall hold your peace" (14:13,14). Had it not been for Moses' previous training, he would not have been able to stand so confidently as God's representative at that time.

Examples of Progressive Strengthening

There are many scriptural examples of individuals who were progressively strengthened. For example, Jacob was overcome at Peniel that he might overcome! Joseph went down to prison before he rose to one of the highest positions in Egypt. Even Christ came down to the cross and then was exalted above every name.

In all of these examples we see the principle stated in John 12:24: "Except a corn of wheat fall into the ground and die, it abideth alone: but if it die, it bringeth forth much fruit." We are also reminded of Revelation 3:21: "To him that overcometh will I grant to sit with me in my throne, even as I also overcame, and am set down with my Father in his throne." It is no wonder that Colossians 3:1-3 tells us: "If [since] ye then be risen with Christ, seek those things which are above, where Christ sitteth on the right hand of God. Set your affection on things above, not on things on the earth. For ye are dead [have died], and your life is hid with Christ in God." The Apostle Paul experienced these truths also. Paul said, "For when I am weak, then am I strong" (II Cor. 12:10). He also stated, "I am crucified with Christ: nevertheless I live; yet not I, but Christ liveth in me: and the life which I now live in the flesh I live by the faith of the Son of God, who loved me, and gave himself for me" (Gal. 2:20).

Thus, it was necessary for Moses to have experienced the disciplining hand of God so that he would be ready for fruit bearing. He was progressively strengthened and was ready for God to begin His real work through him. This is why the Lord was able to tell him, "Now shalt thou see what I will do to Pharaoh" (Ex. 6:1). Moses had been very discouraged by the rejection of his own people, and having come to a complete end of himself, he turned to God. Because of this God was able to announce that His real work with Pharaoh could begin. This was actually the beginning of the end for Egypt, and in a sense it was the beginning of the nation of Israel. Also, it was the beginning of the greatest life ever lived by an individual except Christ Himself.

Some say that life begins at 40, but for Moses life began at 80. The 80 years were required for him to be precisely where God wanted him to be so he could be mightily used. Moses' desire was the same as that later expressed by the Apostle Paul: "That I may know him, and the power of his resurrection, and the fellowship of his sufferings, being made conformable unto his death" (Phil. 3:10).

"I Am the Lord"

For Moses death was the way to life. The pendulum in his life had swung past center. Too often, we want God to move according to our time schedule, but God has His own schedule. Moses was concerned earlier that God would deliver Israel immediately, but God did not choose to do so. What Moses did not realize was that Israel was far from ready to be delivered. Moses had to learn that God is always on time and that He has a purpose for His precise time schedule.

Another important aspect of Moses' progressive strengthening was that he realized that God—the great I

Am—was doing the work. Exodus 6:2-4 records God's words to Moses: "I am the Lord: and I appeared unto Abraham, unto Isaac, and unto Jacob, by the name of God Almighty, but by my name Jehovah was I not known to them. And I have also established my covenant with them, to give them the land of Canaan, the land of their pilgrimage, wherein they were strangers."

Moses saw God in a way that he had never seen Him before—his inner eyes were opened. In the New Testament Paul prayed that believers would have the eyes of their understanding enlightened (Eph. 1:18), for he also was concerned that we might see God in a new way. In another of Paul's prayers, he prayed, "That he would grant you, according to the riches of his glory, to be strengthened with might by his Spirit in the inner man; that Christ may dwell in your hearts by faith; that ye, being rooted and grounded in love, may be able to comprehend with all saints what is the breadth, and length, and depth, and height; and to know the love of Christ, which passeth knowledge, that ye might be filled with all the fulness of God" (3:16-19).

Moses was being prepared for spiritual warfare, and we, also, need to be prepared for it. This is why Paul told us, "Be strong in the Lord, and in the power of his might" (6:10). Note that the strength is "in the Lord," not in us, and that it is the power of "his" might, not ours.

Exodus 6:6-8 records God's renewed commission to Moses in which the original commission was enlarged and strengthened. As previously stated, it included seven "I wills" and was strengthened by the statement, "I am the Lord."

Notice these verses as translated in the Amplified Bible: "Accordingly, say to the Israelites, I am the Lord, and I will bring you out from under the burdens of the Egyptians, and I will free you from their bondage, and I will rescue you with an outstretched arm—with special and vigorous action—and by mighty acts of judgment. And I will take you to Me for a people, and I will be to you a God; and you shall know that it is I, the Lord your God, Who brings you out from under the burdens of the Egyptians. And I will bring you into the land concerning which I lifted up My hand and swore that I would give it to Abraham, Isaac, and Jacob; and I will give it to you for a heritage. I am the Lord [you have the pledge of My changeless omnipotence and faithfulness]."

The foundation was laid for Moses' real spiritual progress—everything had been set on solid bedrock, and Christ was that Rock. All of the experiences that Moses had after that time rested on this sure foundation.

Standing Alone With God

After Moses had cast himself completely on the Lord and the Lord had assured Moses of what He would do, "Moses spake so unto the children of Israel: but they hearkened not unto Moses for anguish of spirit, and for cruel bondage" (Ex. 6:9).

This reaction must have been very hard for a leader like Moses to accept, but it only verified that he had to learn to stand alone with God. Every true leader has to come to the realization that at times he will have to stand alone. The person unwilling to stand alone with God will never be the kind of leader that God wants him to be. God is looking for a person who will be obedient regardless of what others say. Because Moses was learning to stand alone with God, he was making progress in his relationship with God.

Throughout biblical history men have stood alone with God—men like Noah, Abraham, Joseph and Elijah. Although their friends turned against them and they had no one to lean on for support at times, they stood strong for God because they were willing to stand alone. And Moses' successor was no exception. After the death of Moses, Joshua faithfully led the people of Israel, but at the end of his life he presented the people with a decision they had to make. Joshua told the people, "Choose you this day whom ye will serve; . . . but as for me and my house, we will serve the Lord" (Josh. 24:15). Whether we are in a high position of leadership or not, it is important for us to realize that there will be times when we must stand alone with God for the convictions He has given us through His Word.

When Moses received no response from the Israelites, God told him, "Go in, speak unto Pharaoh king of Egypt, that he let the children of Israel go out of his land" (Ex. 6:11). Notice Moses' response to God's command. Although Moses' faith had been growing by leaps and bounds, there is evidence that his faith was still too small. Moses told God, "Behold, the children of Israel have not hearkened unto me; how then shall Pharaoh hear me, who am of uncircumcised lips?" (v. 12).

Moses had not yet gained complete victory over his introspective nature. He was quick to see his deficiencies and was sure that Pharaoh would not listen to him since his own people would not heed his words. But God did not lose patience with Moses; He continued to work with him until Moses gained the complete victory. God knew Moses' heart, and He did not give up on Moses, although others might have.

How well God knew Moses is indicated in Exodus 7:1 where God promised to make Moses "a god to Pharaoh." Imagine, God had more faith in Moses than Moses had in God! As Moses learned to stand alone with God, he was mightily used in His hands and had power over Pharaoh as if he were one of Pharaoh's gods.

As we consider how Moses acted on the authority of God, we are reminded of a privilege we have that even Moses did not have. Since the Day of Pentecost, as recorded in Acts 2, Christ lives within every believer. This is why Colossians 1:27 says, "Christ in you, the hope of glory." Verse 29 reveals that the power of Christ works mightily in each believer. So if we are in God's will when we speak or act, then we speak and act with His authority because He lives within us.

As God was preparing Moses to go before Pharaoh again, He left no room for Moses to falter. God told Moses what would happen when he went before Pharaoh. In His omniscience God saw the future and total victory, but time was an element Moses had to contend with, so he needed patience. Time is always a significant element for man, but it is not for God. God is not a creature of time; He is the Creator of time.

What God has promised concerning Israel will all be fulfilled even though thousands of years have now gone by without the final fulfillment. Although this may cause some to doubt the promises of God, the fulfillment of these promises is not less certain just because much time has elapsed. God is not affected by time.

God told Moses, "I will harden Pharaoh's heart, and multiply my signs and my wonders in the land of Egypt. But Pharaoh shall not harken unto you, that I may lay my hand upon Egypt, and bring forth mine armies, and my people the children of Israel, out of the land of Egypt by great judgments" (Ex. 7:3,4).

God then made this solemn promise to Moses: "And the Egyptians shall know that I am the Lord" (v. 5). All of Egypt would finally know God's sovereign power and would have to submit to Him, even though they would not place their faith in Him. God would eventually prove Himself to be far greater than any of the gods of Egypt.

Total Obedience

Then we read this beautiful statement: "Moses and Aaron did as the Lord commanded them, so did they" (v. 6). They demonstrated total obedience, and it is this kind of obedience that is the key to complete success. Although there were obstacles and Moses and Aaron would have reservations, yet they completely obeyed the Lord.

As we obey the Lord, we will experience success also. The Lord Jesus Christ has told us, "If ye abide in me, and my words abide in you, ye shall ask what ye will, and it shall be done unto you" (John 15:7). Note what this verse really says. The words "if ye abide in me" indicate complete trust and commitment to Him. We are to get our orders from Him—"and my words abide in you." Then, and only then, is it true that "ye shall ask what ye will, and it shall be done unto you." This is the key to spiritual success.

This reminds us of what God told Joshua: "Only be thou strong and very courageous, that thou mayest observe to do according to all the law, which Moses my servant commanded thee: turn not from it to the right hand or to the left, that thou mayest prosper whithersoever thou goest. This book of the law shall not depart out of thy mouth; but thou shalt meditate therein day and night, that thou mayest observe to do according to all that is written therein: for then thou shalt make thy way prosperous, and then thou shalt have good success" (Josh. 1:7,8).

But the Bible contains many examples of those who did not obey the Lord completely. Perhaps one of the best examples is Saul, the first king of Israel. Through Samuel the prophet God had instructed Saul to completely destroy the Amalekites and all of their possessions. Yet, Saul went against God's clear instructions and spared the best of the livestock, as well as the king of the Amalekites. When Samuel faced Saul with his disobedience to the Lord, Saul blamed his people for taking the best of the livestock, but he explained that it was so they could make sacrifices to the Lord (see I Sam. 15:21). Think of it. Saul had disobeyed the Lord and was going to use what he had gained in his disobedience to make a sacrifice to the Lord! Samuel told Saul, "Hath the Lord as great delight in burnt-offerings and sacrifices, as in obeying the voice of the Lord? Behold, to obey is better than sacrifice, and to hearken than the fat of rams" (v. 22).

Moses went before Pharaoh, and from this point forward we see unquestioned obedience on his part. Total obedience is really recognition of God's absolute sovereignty, and this is what Moses finally recognized.

The complete obedience of Moses is also seen in Exodus 7:10: "And Moses and Aaron went in unto Pharaoh, and they did so as the Lord had commanded." Verse 20 emphasizes the same theme: "And Moses and Aaron did so, as the Lord commanded." Twelve times God gave the orders, and twelve times Moses and Aaron did as God said. Miracles began to happen one after another as they gave unquestioned obedience to the Lord.

This teaches us that we must be where God wants us to be at the time He wants us to be there, and we must do what He says, if we expect to see things happen. As the believer desires to act and obey, he will see God work mightily in and through him.

Moses' Increased Boldness

It is interesting to see how Moses' faith continued to grow. This was especially apparent during the plague of the frogs that, through Moses and Aaron, had been brought on Egypt because of Pharaoh's refusal to let the people go. "Moses said to Pharaoh, 'The honor is yours to tell me: when shall I entreat for you and your servants and your people, that the frogs be destroyed from you and your houses, that they may be left only in the Nile?' Then he said, 'Tomorrow.' So he said, 'May it be according to your word, that you may know that there is no one like the Lord our God. And the frogs will depart from you and your houses and your servants and your people; they will be left only in the Nile' " (Ex. 8:9-11, NASB).

Moses was becoming bolder as he spoke to Pharaoh. Moses knew the Lord intimately, and he was walking with the Lord, so he was bold in speaking to Pharaoh about these matters. It is not enough just to have faith; one must act on his faith. True faith produces boldness.

Many times I'm reminded of this as I pray about a certain matter. I tell the Lord what I need or what I feel might be done, and then the Lord seems to say to me, "Will you tell Me to do it?" Telling the Lord, in faith, to do something is far different than asking for a particular matter. Mark 11:22,23 gives us the basis for telling the Lord to do something for us. These verses say, "Jesus answering saith unto them, Have faith in God. For verily I say unto you, That whosoever shall say unto this mountain, Be thou removed, and be thou cast into the sea; and shall not doubt in his heart, but shall believe that those things which he saith shall come to pass; he shall have whatsoever he saith." Notice that we are not to ask the mountain to move; we are to tell it to move. When our faith is based on a definite promise of God, He desires that we tell Him to do certain things for us.

As Moses spoke to Pharaoh about the frogs, he said, "Be it according to thy word: that thou mayest know that there is none like unto the Lord our God" (Ex. 8:10). Moses had only one purpose in mind, and that was to glorify God. Moses sought to honor God alone, and this is why God used him so mightily.

Because Moses and Aaron had been completely obedient to the Lord's command, the Lord responded to Moses' prayer. The Bible says, "And Moses and Aaron went out from Pharaoh: and Moses cried unto the Lord because of the frogs which he had brought against Pharaoh. And the Lord did according to the word of Moses; and the frogs died out of the houses, out of the villages, and out of the fields" (vv.

12,13). Because Moses had obeyed the word of the Lord, the Lord acted according to the word of Moses. The Lord loves to act in behalf of the person who dares to believe Him, who dares to venture out in faith, seeking only to glorify God.

Second Chronicles 20 records a striking example of how the Lord responds to those who glorify Him. Jehoshaphat was surrounded by enemies, and he prayed earnestly to the Lord. The Lord made it clear to him that he would not have to really fight the battle, for He told him, "The battle is not your's, but God's" (v. 15). Jehoshaphat took God at His word and put singers in front of his army as it went to meet the enemy. As the singers offered praise to Him, God miraculously worked in behalf of Israel.

It is important, however, that we guard against presumption—we must not expect Him to do something when He has not specifically indicated that it is His will to do so. But when we have done God's will and seek only to glorify Him, we can be bold in our prayer life. Jesus told the Father, "I have glorified thee on the earth; I have finished the work which thou gavest me to do" (John 17:4). Psalm 37:4 promises, "Delight thyself also in the Lord; and he shall give thee the desires of thine heart." If we have God in first place in our lives, we may be confident that He will act in our behalf.

The Weakening of Pharaoh

As the plagues came on Pharaoh and the Egyptians, he began to weaken a little bit. We will later study the plagues in detail, but at this point we want to especially notice how Moses was strengthened along the way. At one point during the plagues Pharaoh said to Moses, "Go, sacrifice to your God [here] in the land [of Egypt]. And Moses said, It is not suitable or right to do that; for the animals the Egyptians hold sacred and will not permit to be slain, are those which we are accustomed to sacrifice to the Lord our God; if we did this before the eyes of the Egyptians, would they not stone us? We will go three days' journey into the wilderness and sacrifice to the Lord our God, as He will command us" (Ex. 8:25-27, Amplified).

This was Pharaoh's first offer, but Moses was bold in faith and refused to compromise. Moses spoke for God and completely refused anything less than what God demanded. Moses even exposed Pharaoh's false religion as he mentioned that the Egyptians held certain animals to be sacred. Moses made it clear that his firm intention was to obey God completely.

That Moses' faith was becoming bolder and bolder is also seen in that he prayed for an end to the plague of flies: "Moses went out from Pharaoh, and intreated the Lord. And the Lord did according to the word of Moses; and he removed the swarms of flies from Pharaoh, from his servants, and from his people; there remained not one" (vv. 30,31). This was not presumption on Moses' part because he already had assurance from God that such a prayer was in accordance with His will.

Consider another incident from chapter 9. Moses had announced that a great hailstorm was coming and that everything not under a roof would be destroyed. Verses 20 and 21 say, "He that feared the word of the Lord among the servants of Pharaoh made his servants and his cattle flee into the houses: and he that regarded not the word of the Lord left his servants and his cattle in the field." These verses indicate that a number of people were taking Moses at his word, even though the majority still refused to believe the word of God through Moses.

This is a good lesson to us—when people see God working in us, they will begin to believe His Word. This is why the Lord Jesus Christ said, "Let your light so shine before men, that they may see your good works, and glorify your Father which is in heaven" (Matt. 5:16).

Exodus 9:29,30 records another incident of Moses' growing in boldness. He stated what he would ask God for, with complete confidence that it would take place as he said. Concerning the plague of the hailstorm, Moses told Pharaoh, "As soon as I am gone out of the city, I will spread abroad my hands unto the Lord; and the thunder shall cease, neither shall there be any more hail; that thou mayest know how that the earth is the Lord's. But as for thee and thy servants, I know that ye will not yet fear the Lord God." Moses' attitude toward prayer reminds us of Matthew 7:7: "Ask, and it shall be given you; seek, and ye shall find; knock, and it shall be opened unto you."

Was Moses' faith rewarded? The answer is found in Exodus 9:33: "And Moses went out of the city from Pharaoh, and spread abroad his hands unto the Lord: and the thunders and hail ceased, and the rain was not poured upon the earth."

Moses obeyed God to the letter even though he knew Pharaoh would have a negative response to everything he said. Moses had learned to believe God completely; he had learned that God has a program of progress. Moses and Aaron's obedience is again seen in Exodus 10:1-3: "And the Lord said unto Moses, Go in unto Pharaoh: for I have hardened his heart, and the heart of his servants, that I might shew these my signs before him: and that thou mayest tell in the ears of thy son, and of thy son's son, what things I have wrought in Egypt, and my signs which I have done among them; that ye may know how that I am the Lord. And Moses and Aaron came in unto Pharaoh, and said unto him, Thus saith the Lord God of the Hebrews, How long wilt thou refuse to humble thyself before me? Let my people go, that they may serve me."

Exodus 10:9,10 reveals that Pharaoh offered another compromise, but Moses boldly rejected it. In answer to Pharaoh's question concerning who would go into the wilderness to worship, Moses said, "We will go with our young and with our old, with our sons and with our daughters, with our flocks and with our herds will we go; for we must hold a feast unto the Lord" (v. 9). Then Pharaoh replied, "Let the Lord be so with you, as I will let you go, and your little ones: look to it; for evil is before you" (v. 10). Moses insisted on doing precisely what the Lord had instructed him to do. He would not leave anyone behind as they went into the wilderness to worship.

Verse 24 reveals another of Pharaoh's offers—he urged Moses to let the flocks and herds remain in Egypt while the people went into the wilderness to worship. Again, Moses steadfastly refused to compromise.

Pharaoh finally became so angered at Moses that he said to him, "Get thee from me, take heed to thyself, see my face no more; for in that day thou seest my face thou shalt die"

(v. 28). Moses solemnly responded, "Thou hast spoken well, I will see thy face again no more" (v. 29). In spite of the fact that Moses was driven from Pharaoh's presence, he became bolder in his faith and seemed to realize that God was about through with Pharaoh. As indicated previously, it seems that Pharaoh had weakened some along the way, but he still bitterly opposed God. Pharaoh was unaware at this time that his own life was hanging in the balance.

The Greatness of Moses

Although Moses was God's instrument in bringing plagues on Egypt, the Egyptians gained more and more respect for Moses and the Israelites. The Bible says, "The Lord gave the people favour in the sight of the Egyptians. Moreover the man Moses was very great in the land of Egypt, in the sight of Pharaoh's servants, and in the sight of the people" (Ex. 11:3). So although Moses did not gain favor before Pharaoh, he did before Pharaoh's people.

The greatness of Moses is indicated in that the Bible refers to him at least 826 times. Thus, we see that his faith and obedience won him a significant place in God's hall of fame.

Although Pharaoh was so angry at Moses that he threatened to kill him if he saw him again, Moses gave a final pronouncement from God before leaving: "Thus saith the Lord, About midnight will I go out into the midst of Egypt: and all the firstborn in the land of Egypt shall die, from the firstborn of Pharaoh that sitteth upon his throne, even unto the firstborn of the maidservant that is behind the mill; and all the firstborn of beasts. And there shall be a great cry throughout all the land of Egypt, such as there was none like it, nor shall be like it any more" (vv. 4-6).

Moses was fearless because he spoke for God. Proverbs 16:7 says, "When a man's ways please the Lord, he maketh even his enemies to be at peace with him." Because Moses was in the center of God's will, Pharaoh was unable to harm him. This reminds us of Elijah, who fearlessly stood before wicked Ahab and later killed the prophets of Baal. No one was able to touch Elijah's life because God was protecting him. And during the future Tribulation two witnesses will

appear whom the Antichrist will hate, but he will not be able
to do anything to them until God permits it.

So we see how Moses was strengthened to the extent that
he could fearlessly proclaim this great judgment on all of
Egypt. But notice how God evidenced His blessing on the
Israelites. Moses said, "But against any of the sons of Israel a
dog shall not even bark, whether against man or beast, that
you may understand how the Lord makes a distinction
between Egypt and Israel" (Ex. 11:7, NASB). What a bold
prophecy this was! The Israelites numbered about three
million at this time, and one can imagine all the commotion
they would cause in making final preparations to flee Egypt.
They would have to quickly gather all of their possessions,
and their animals would have to be herded together, yet no
dog would even bark at them! God shut their mouths as He
shut the lions' mouths for Daniel.

Notice especially the reason that God prevented the dogs
from barking at the Israelites—it was to be a sign to the
Egyptians: "That ye may know how that the Lord doth put a
difference between the Egyptians and Israel." Verse 8 says,
"And all these thy servants shall come down unto me, and
bow down themselves unto me, saying, Get thee out, and all
the people that follow thee: and after that I will go out. And
he went out from Pharaoh in a great anger."

Moses had a genuine faith in God's purpose and program,
and this produced a holy indignation against those who dared
try to thwart God. Moses' early timidity contrasts greatly
with the boldness he evidenced at this time. Earlier, he was
sure he was not the man for God to send, but later he stood
before Pharaoh and fearlessly pronounced God's judgment,
even though Pharaoh had threatened his life.

What made all this difference? Moses knew he was in the
will of God, so he had no fear of man. Concerning this matter
Psalm 56 is of much encouragement to us. The psalmist said,
"In God I will praise his word, in God I have put my trust; I
will not fear what flesh can do unto me. . . . In God have I
put my trust: I will not be afraid what man can do unto me"
(vv. 4,11).

A key to Moses' boldness is also found in Hebrews 11:27:
"By faith he forsook Egypt, not fearing the wrath of the
king: for he endured, as seeing him who is invisible." That is

it! Because Moses saw Him who is invisible—God—he did not fear Pharaoh. Moses knew that God's honor was at stake, so he refused to cower before Pharaoh.

Moses evidenced holy indignation because of Pharaoh's persistent arrogance, deceit, cruelty and impiety against God. Having left the presence of Pharaoh, the Lord told Moses and Aaron, "This month shall be unto you the beginning of months: it shall be the first month of the year to you" (Ex. 12:2). This chapter records God's instituting of the Passover. Nothing like it had ever happened before. But even though they had no previous experience, Moses and the Israelites faithfully carried out God's instructions to the last detail. Hebrews 11:28 says of Moses, "Through faith he kept the passover, and the sprinkling of blood, lest he that destroyed the firstborn should touch them."

Moses had the complete respect of his people at this point. All three million of them were ready to follow him. They did not really know where they were going, but they had confidence that Moses knew. He gained their complete confidence because he demonstrated complete faith and obedience.

Beginning the Journey

The response of the Israelites to the explicit instructions concerning the Passover is seen in Exodus 12:27,28: "The people bowed the head and worshipped. And the children of Israel went away, and did as the Lord had commanded Moses and Aaron, so did they." This was another indication of the confidence the Israelites had in Moses—a confidence so great they were willing to follow him even though they did not know what lay ahead.

But the first real test for them came after they had barely started on their way—they were going a different direction than they had expected! The shortest route from northern Egypt, where they were living, to the land of Canaan was only about a three-day journey, but they were going in another direction. They were going south toward the Red Sea. God had a reason for this, however.

Exodus 13:17,18 says, "It came to pass, when Pharaoh had let the people go, that God led them not through the way of the land of the Philistines, although that was near; for God said, Lest peradventure the people repent when they see war, and they return to Egypt: but God led the people about, through the way of the wilderness of the Red sea: and the children of Israel went up harnessed out of the land of Egypt." Even though the way seemed wrong to the people and may have seemed strange to Moses, God was working to accomplish His will. He was working on the heart of Pharaoh, on the hearts of the Israelites and in the heart of Moses. As far as Israel was concerned, God was working all things together for good—they were experiencing the truth stated later in Romans 8:28.

Moses had increased in faith to the extent that he did not question God about this detour. But as the Israelites went further, they came to an impasse; they were completely hemmed in. The pursuing Egyptians were behind them, mountains and marshes were on either side of them, and the Red Sea was ahead of them.

Exodus 14:10 says, "And when Pharaoh drew nigh, the children of Israel lifted up their eyes, and, behold, the Egyptians marched after them; and they were sore afraid: and the children of Israel cried out unto the Lord." They were gripped with fear at this point because they could not see any possibility of deliverance. In their despair they said to Moses, "Because there were no graves in Egypt, hast thou taken us away to die in the wilderness? Wherefore hast thou dealt thus with us, to carry us forth out of Egypt? Is not this the word that we did tell thee in Egypt, saying, Let us alone, that we may serve the Egyptians? For it had been better for us to serve the Egyptians, than that we should die in the wilderness" (vv. 11,12). Death seemed imminent to the Israelites, and in the face of it they expressed bitter feelings toward Moses.

Although Moses had not received any new orders from God, his faith was unshaken. Moses did not falter at this point even though he obviously could not humanly see any way out. We now realize why God took so much time and exercised so much patience in training His man. Moses had complete confidence that God knew what He was doing. Moses realized it was God's business to lead, and it was his business to believe and obey.

So Moses told the people, "Fear ye not, stand still, and see the salvation of the Lord, which he will shew to you to day: for the Egyptians whom ye have seen to day, ye shall see them again no more for ever. The Lord shall fight for you, and ye shall hold your peace" (vv. 13,14).

Imagine making a statement like that without any direct orders from God! Moses did not know precisely where they were going or what they would do, but his faith in God was unshakable. He did not falter, even when the people turned against him again. Their faith was weak, but his was strong because of the training he had received from God.

Notice how God responded to Moses after such a demonstration of faith: "Wherefore criest thou unto me? Speak unto the children of Israel, that they go forward" (v. 15). What orders! Remember, they were hemmed in on all sides, yet God commanded them to go forward. But Moses had such faith in God that when God said to go forward, Moses went forward. But what about the Red Sea?

God told Moses, "Lift thou up thy rod, and stretch out thine hand over the sea, and divide it: and the children of Israel shall go on dry ground through the midst of the sea" (v. 16). These were the detailed instructions concerning how they were to go forward, but there first had to be the willingness to go forward simply because God had commanded it. Moses was willing to go forward with God, so God then gave him the detailed instructions. If we are not willing to move forward with God, we need not expect that He will give us instructions.

God went on to explain to Moses, "And I, behold, I will harden the hearts of the Egyptians, and they shall follow them: and I will get me honour upon Pharaoh, and upon all his host, upon his chariots, and upon his horsemen. And the Egyptians shall know that I am the Lord" (vv. 17,18).

Moses trusted God, and God did not let him down. Forty years earlier, relying on mere human strength, Moses had killed one Egyptian, but by faith he was now about to destroy all of Egypt.

Think of the lesson we can learn from this. Through the death of the Lord Jesus Christ, He not only procured our salvation, but He also destroyed the power that Satan has over us (Heb. 2:14). Because the power has been broken, we may now resist Satan in the power of Christ (I Pet. 5:6-9; James 4:7). That the Lord Jesus Christ has overcome the power of the world is seen in His words: "In the world ye shall have tribulation: but be of good cheer; I have overcome the world" (John 16:33).

Moses' Obedience; Israel's Escape

So Moses did what God told him to do—he stretched out his hand over the Red Sea, and the Lord caused the water to divide so the Israelites could walk through (Ex. 14:21). God delivered His people as Moses had faith to take Him at His word!

Notice the response of the Israelites after they had been delivered: "Thus the Lord saved Israel that day from the hand of the Egyptians. . . . And when Israel saw the great power which the Lord had used against the Egyptians, the people feared the Lord, and they believed in the Lord and in His servant Moses" (vv. 30,31, NASB). This is exactly what God wanted them to do. Israel was saved that day as it was united, or identified, with Moses.

This fact is emphasized in the New Testament. The Apostle Paul said, "Moreover, brethren, I would not that ye should be ignorant, how that all our fathers were under the cloud, and all passed through the sea; and were all baptized unto Moses in the cloud and in the sea" (I Cor. 10:1,2). Here we see that the word "baptized" does not always involve water, for these Israelites did not even get wet! The basic element involved in baptism is identification. Only as the Israelites were identified with Moses could they expect deliverance by God. In the New Testament water baptism shows one's identification with Jesus Christ as personal Saviour.

Then came the song of victory for the Israelites. It surely must have been prepared earlier because they were able to sing it as soon as they saw the judgment of God on the Egyptians and realized the great deliverance they had experienced. I personally think that Moses must have previously written this song, which is recorded in Exodus 15. At this point, Israel's faith looked beyond the Red Sea and Egypt all the way to Canaan.

Consider the spiritual growth Moses had experienced. His first 40 years were spent primarily in the courts of Egypt learning the basics. The next 40 years were spent in the desert learning to know God intimately. Then the experiences of the next year perfected his faith in God as he faced Pharaoh and led the Israelites out of Egypt. This proves that it takes time to know God. The longer Moses walked with the Lord, the more he increased in faith.

Chapter 4

God's Strategy for Deliverance

At this point, let us reconsider some of the plagues, emphasizing how God outlined His stategy of delivering Israel from Egypt.

It was immediately apparent that the king would greatly resist letting the Israelites go. The purpose of the plagues was stated in Exodus 3. God told Moses, "I am sure that the king of Egypt will not let you go, no, not by a mighty hand. And I will stretch out my hand, and smite Egypt with all my wonders which I will do in the midst thereof: and after that he will let you go" (vv. 19,20).

For many years the Egyptians had oppressed Israel, and God had allowed it, but the time had come for Him to act in behalf of His chosen people. God was going to take vengeance on those who had made slaves of the Israelites. But before He exercised vengeance, God displayed mercy. Thus, God outlined His strategy of a series of ten plagues.

The Egyptians were acquainted with many unpleasant natural phenomena, but they were to see a tremendous, supernatural demonstration in the announced series of afflictions. In fact, almost all—if not every one—of the plagues were aimed directly at one of their gods. Each plague came with an intensity they had never experienced before. The first three plagues affected both Israel and Egypt, but the last seven were geographically located so that the Israelites, who lived in northern Egypt, were not affected.

Moses not only predicted each plague, but each plague came to an end only when he used his God-given power to remove it. Such predictions have never been duplicated even with our modern weather satellites and electronic computers.

Moses was 100 percent accurate because he was announcing what God told him.

And besides this, Moses even announced that God would protect His own people in Goshen, thus showing the superior power of the God of Israel over the gods of Egypt. The Egyptians thought their gods were the greatest, but they soon realized that their gods were nothing before the eternal God.

The Purpose of the Plagues

The plagues served at least five distinct purposes. First, they gave a public demonstration of the mighty power of the Lord God. Even the magicians, who were Pharaoh's wise men, acknowledged this fact. When they were unable to produce lice as Moses and Aaron did, the magicians said to Pharaoh, "This is the finger of God" (Ex. 8:19). They admitted that it was a miracle far above anything they could perform.

Second, the plagues were the divine visitation of wrath; that is, they were a punishment of Pharaoh and his people for their cruel treatment of Israel. When the horrible plague of locusts came on Egypt, Pharaoh admitted his shameful treatment of Israel when he said to Moses, "I have sinned against the Lord your God, and against you. Now therefore forgive, I pray thee, my sin only this once, and intreat the Lord your God, that he may take away from me this death only" (10:16,17).

Third, the plagues were a judgment of God on the gods of Egypt. The gods of Egypt were really demons. Concerning the tenth and most severe plague, God said, "For I will pass through the land of Egypt this night, and will smite all the firstborn in the land of Egypt, both man and beast; and against all the gods of Egypt I will execute judgment: I am the Lord" (12:12).

Fourth, the plagues were a solemn warning to other nations that God would curse those who cursed Israel. When God first called Abraham and promised to make a nation of him, God told him, "I will bless them that bless thee, and curse him that curseth thee: and in thee shall all families of the earth be blessed" (Gen. 12:3).

After the Israelites had been delivered from Egypt and were finally ready to enter the land of Canaan, they sent spies into Jericho. There the spies met Rahab, the harlot, who told them, "I know that the Lord hath given you the land, and that your terror is fallen upon us, and that all the inhabitants of the land faint because of you. For we have heard how the Lord dried up the water of the Red sea for you, when ye came out of Egypt; and what ye did unto the two kings of the Amorites, that were on the other side Jordan, Sihon and Og, whom ye utterly destroyed. And as soon as we had heard these things, our hearts did melt, neither did there remain any more courage in any man, because of you: for the Lord your God, he is God in heaven above, and in earth beneath" (Josh. 2:9-11).

The Philistines had also heard about the plagues God brought on Egypt, as indicated by I Samuel 4:7,8: "The Philistines were afraid, for they said, God is come into the camp. And they said, Woe unto us! For there hath not been such a thing heretofore. Woe unto us! Who shall deliver us out of the hand of these mighty Gods? These are the Gods that smote the Egyptians with all the plagues in the wilderness."

Fifth, the plagues on Egypt also served as a series of testings for Israel while the nation was in Egypt. This fact is indicated by what Moses later asked the people: "Did ever people hear the voice of God speaking out of the midst of the fire, as thou hast heard, and live? Or hath God assayed to go and take him a nation from the midst of another nation, by temptations, by signs, and by wonders, and by war, and by a mighty hand, and by a stretched out arm, and by great terrors, according to all that the Lord your God did for you in Egypt before your eyes? Unto thee it was shewed, that thou mightest know that the Lord he is God; there is none else beside him" (Deut. 4:33-35).

Although the trials and burdens they experienced in Egypt were difficult for Israel to bear, when they had been delivered through the Red Sea, they were able to admit, "Who is like unto thee, O Lord, among the gods? Who is like thee, glorious in holiness, fearful in praises, doing wonders?" (Ex. 15:11).

The Arrangement of the Plagues

The arrangement of the plagues refers to the way they are grouped together—nine of the ten plagues are arranged in three groups of three plagues each. The severity of the divine judgment increased in intensity with each group of plagues.

The first group of three plagues interfered primarily with the comfort of Egypt. Israel also experienced these discomforts in the land of Goshen. The first plague affected the water by turning it into blood, leaving no water to drink. The second was an invasion of frogs that got into everything. The third was an invasion of lice. What a discomfort!

The second group of three plagues was primarily directed against the possessions of the Egyptians. The Israelites were exempted from these plagues (Ex. 8:22,23). There were swarms of insects that afflicted men and animals. Next, there was an epidemic disease that killed many cattle. The third plague in this group produced boils on men and animals.

The third group of three plagues was far more severe and brought desolation and death. There was hail and thunder, and fire was running along the earth, destroying everything in its course. There were locusts that consumed everything that was left. And there was darkness that could be felt—possibly a black dust storm.

The tenth plague, although last in order, was announced first when God gave Moses instructions about going before Pharaoh (4:23). This last plague had special significance to the Israelites, because it related to their redemption.

Plagues Establish the Faith of Israel

For 400 years the Israelites had been in a strange land of strange gods. These gods were revealed through the magicians, who were able to perform satanic deeds. The supernatural power of the magicians came from the demons who energized them. But most of the plagues that Moses and Aaron brought about could not be imitated by the magicians. So, in a sense, the plagues were instrumental in establishing the Israelites in a true knowledge of Almighty God in this land of strange gods. The true God revealed Himself in power so Israel would recognize not only His existence but also His omnipotence.

The Scriptures indicate that the Israelites had backslidden while in Egypt and that some were even worshiping the gods of the Egyptians. They still had this tendency even after they were delivered from Egypt, because later they made and worshiped a golden calf (Ex. 32:1-6). No doubt the calf was even related to their experience in Egypt because the Egyptians worshiped cattle.

But as the Israelites were in Egypt, they saw—by means of the plagues—the impotency of the false gods of Egypt and the omnipotence of the Lord God of Israel. Although the Israelites were affected by the first three plagues, they were delivered from the other ones. Inasmuch as God delivered them from the remaining plagues, He revealed Himself to Israel as God Almighty—He was able to do all things. He also revealed Himself to them as the Lord God—the ever-present God to help.

God revealed to the Israelites that the gods of the Egyptians could not stand before Him. This was seen especially in the first miracle performed before Pharaoh. Aaron threw down his staff, and it became a serpent (7:10). Pharaoh then called his wise men, and they threw down their staffs, and they became serpents. But the power of the true God over the false gods was demonstrated when Aaron's staff-turned-serpent swallowed up the staffs-turned-serpents of Pharaoh's wise men (v. 12).

Just as the power of the true God was seen to be much greater than that of the false gods of Egypt, so today we need to recognize that the power of God is much greater than that of Satan. In fact, Satan is actually a defeated foe. When the Lord Jesus Christ died on the cross, He broke the power of Satan, just as God broke the power of Egypt over the Israelites.

However, just as the nation of Egypt still existed even though it did not have such power, so Satan still exists even though his power has been broken. Satan attempts to gain power over the Christian, but no believer needs to yield to Satan's enticements. James 4:7 instructs: "Submit yourselves therefore to God. Resist the devil, and he will flee from you." The order is significant in this verse: first, "submit yourselves therefore to God"; second, "resist the devil, and he will flee from you." Since Satan is actually a defeated foe, we need to take a definite stand against anything he attempts to do in our lives.

As Aaron and Moses performed miracles before Pharaoh, the magicians of Egypt were allowed to demonstrate their powers on three different occasions. First, as we have seen, they threw down their staffs, and they turned into serpents just as Aaron's did (Ex. 7:10-13). Second, the magicians of Egypt were able to turn water into blood even as Aaron did (vv. 20-22). Third, the magicians of Egypt were able to bring forth frogs as Aaron did (8:1-7). Just as the frogs were not clean, so this reminds us that Satan's work is one of uncleanness.

Let us not overestimate Satan; he is able to perform the unusual, but his power cannot compare with the power of Almighty God. The most basic thing to realize about Satan is that he is an imitator. He desires to imitate God and God's power. This is demonstrated by the three miracles which the magicians of Egypt imitated by the power of Satan. Just as in the biblical parable where Satan sows tares among the wheat (Matt. 13:24,25), so Pharaoh sought to nullify the miracles of the true God by having his wise men imitate Aaron's miracles.

Satan is still at work today, imitating miracles with subtle methods and wiles of deceit. The Bible tells us, "Your adversary the devil, as a roaring lion, walketh about, seeking whom he may devour" (I Pet. 5:8). The Bible also tells us that Satan appears as "an angel of light" (II Cor. 11:14). We must remember that what seems right on the surface may simply be a tactic of Satan to draw us off the course of pleasing God in all that we do.

Because Satan's desire is to imitate the genuine work of God, we need much discernment. Thus, those who teach false doctrine and thereby are followers of Satan are those who have a form of godliness but deny the power of true godliness (II Tim. 3:5). Such people are also those who are "ever learning, and never able to come to the knowledge of the truth" (v. 7).

The plagues brought on the Egyptians by God furnish a striking prophetic forecast of God's judgment during the coming Tribulation. Revelation 8—16 tells of these judgments. As God and Moses were vindicated in Egypt, so the Lord Jesus Christ will be vindicated in the end time. The Apostle John wrote: "I saw heaven opened, and behold a white horse; and he that sat upon him was called Faithful and True, and in righteousness he doth judge and make war. . . . And out of his mouth goeth a sharp sword, that with it he should smite the nations: and he shall rule them with a rod of iron: and he treadeth the winepress of the fierceness and wrath of Almighty God. And he hath on his vesture and on his thigh a name written, King of Kings, and Lord of Lords" (Rev. 19:11,15,16).

Chapter 5

The Progressive Hardening
of Pharaoh's Heart

Four verses on the subject of the hardening of Pharaoh's heart are especially significant. As God was instructing Moses about going before Pharaoh, He told Moses, "I am sure that the king of Egypt will not let you go, no, not by a mighty hand" (Ex. 3:19). We observe from this verse that the omniscient God already knew the outcome.

Verse 20 reveals how God planned to counteract Pharaoh's refusal: "I will stretch out my hand, and smite Egypt with all my wonders which I will do in the midst thereof: and after that he will let you go." So while God told Moses that Pharaoh would not let the people go, He also explained how He planned to deal with Pharaoh.

God's announcement to Moses that He would harden Pharaoh's heart was first recorded in Exodus 4:21: "When thou goest to return into Egypt, see that thou do all those wonders before Pharaoh, which I have put in thine hand: but I will harden his heart, that he shall not let the people go." What a statement! These strong words have generated much discussion among Bible students. As we examine this subject, let us remember that this statement was made in the same context in which God told Moses what to say to Pharaoh: "I say unto thee, Let my son go, that he may serve me: and if thou refuse to let him go, behold, I will slay thy son, even thy firstborn" (v. 23). Thus, we see that the hardening of Pharaoh's heart was mentioned in connection with Pharaoh's absolute refusal to let Israel go, and this refusal brought the final plague.

51

God's Will and God's Nature

The question arises: Does God use His sovereignty and omnipotence to destroy anything that comes in His way? In answering this question, we must first consider God's will concerning the salvation of mankind. First Timothy 2:4 says of God, "Who will have all men to be saved, and to come unto the knowledge of the truth." So what does God want? He wants everyone to be saved.

This same truth is seen in II Peter 3:9: "The Lord is not slack concerning his promise, as some men count slackness; but is longsuffering to us-ward, not willing that any should perish, but that all should come to repentance." Here again we see that it is God's will that people be saved, and we can count on the fact that God will not do anything contrary to His own will.

Another important question is, What is God like? That is, What is His nature? His nature is to love, and John 3:16 highlights this aspect of His nature. Although God could use His sovereignty to punish and to destroy, He chooses rather to use His sovereignty to win others to Himself through exercising much longsuffering and mercy. But if His love is refused, God will exercise His sovereignty to eternally punish those who reject Him.

The Hardened Heart

As we consider the hardening of Pharaoh's heart, we must also consider what was meant by the individual Hebrew words that are translated "harden" or "hardening" in the King James Version. Three different Hebrew words were used, but they are similar in meaning. They basically mean "to be or become strong," "to strengthen or harden," "to make heavy or hard" and "to make sharp or hard."

Various translations render these words differently—"to render obstinate," "to make stubborn" or "to make strong." From these words and the translations of them we see that Pharaoh's feelings and attitudes were to become firm—they would not change. "To make strong" seems to be a primary meaning of the words involved. Pharaoh became strong in his feelings and attitudes against God. Foolhardiness is also implied by these words in that a strong-willed or strong-minded person often does things that are contrary to reason. Pharaoh was insensitive to any possible judgment that would result from the strong position he took.

Having considered this matter carefully, I believe that Pharaoh hardened his own heart, and then God hardened it further. Pharaoh first made his own heart hard, and then God confirmed, or further hardened, him in the position he had taken against God. It was as if the Lord were saying, "I will make Pharaoh's heart firm so that it will not move; his feelings and attitude toward Me and Israel will not change."

The hardening of Pharaoh's heart is ascribed to God ten times in the Book of Exodus. The verses indicate that God not only foreknew and foretold the hardening of Pharaoh's heart, but He also caused or effected it. On the other hand, it is stated just as often that Pharaoh hardened his own heart; that is, he made it strong, or firm. So we see that the hardening of Pharaoh's heart was just as much his own act as that of God's decree.

The progressive hardening of Pharaoh's heart needs to be traced from his first meeting with Moses and Aaron to the overthrowing of his army at the Red Sea. We have already referred to Exodus 3:19,20 and 4:21,23. In these verses we have seen that the Lord announced to Moses what he could expect when he went before Pharaoh. The key to understanding the hardening of Pharaoh's heart is found in Exodus 5:2: "Pharaoh said, Who is the Lord, that I should obey his voice to let Israel go? I know not the Lord, neither will I let Israel go." With these words Pharaoh exposed his rebellious attitude toward God. It is nowhere indicated that God had hardened Pharaoh's heart before this time. The Lord had told Moses, "I will harden his heart" (4:21), but this refers to a future time, and I believe it was after Pharaoh took his strong position as recorded in 5:2.

Through Moses, God had addressed Pharaoh when He gave the mandate, "Let my people go, that they may hold a feast unto me in the wilderness" (5:1). God gave Pharaoh an opportunity to obey; He addressed him in grace and did not at that time announce his judgments or bring them on the haughty king and his subjects.

Before God deals in wrath, He acts in mercy. This has always been God's way, and it is still the way of God today. There are many biblical illustrations of this. Before the world flood of Noah's time, God gave mankind 120 years of warning. Also, before the Israelites went into capitivity, God sent prophets who warned again and again that His judgment would fall if the people did not depart from their sin. God's compassion is especially seen in the words of the Lord Jesus Christ as He wept over Jerusalem: "O Jerusalem, Jerusalem, thou that killest the prophets, and stonest them which are sent unto thee, how often would I have gathered thy children together, even as a hen gathereth her chickens under her wings, and ye would not!" (Matt. 23:37).

How thankful we should be for the mercy of the Lord! Lamentations 3:22,23 expresses it in these words: "It is of the Lord's mercies that we are not consumed, because his compassions fail not. They are new every morning: great is thy faithfulness."

God's Judgment

Because Pharaoh determinedly resisted the sovereign will of God, God eventually had to turn him over to what might be called "judicial blindness." Proverbs 29:1 is applicable to a person such as Pharaoh: "He, that being often reproved hardeneth his neck, shall suddenly be destroyed, and that without remedy." God is absolutely fair in all of His dealings, and He gives sufficient opportunity for a person to repent, but He will not withhold the judgment of sin forever.

The New Testament tells of the judgment which the Lord Jesus Christ will bring on those who reject Him as Saviour. Referring to the judgment He will administer when He returns to earth, II Thessalonians 1:8,9 says, "In flaming fire taking vengeance on them that know not God, and that obey not the gospel of our Lord Jesus Christ: who shall be punished with everlasting destruction from the presence of the Lord, and from the glory of his power." How awful it is to reject God's grace!

Pharaoh was not able to escape judgment when he rejected God's grace, and neither is any other person able to do so. Be aware of the results of rejecting God. To resist the light results in increased darkness. To turn from the truth is to come more and more under the power of the archliar, Satan himself. Pharaoh was so dominated by the archliar that he not only rejected God's command, but he also referred to the command as "vain words" (Ex. 5:9).

Romans 1 sets forth the principle that the one who rejects the grace of God will eventually himself be rejected by God. "Because that which is known about God is evident within them; for God made it evident to them. For since the creation of the world His invisible attributes, His eternal power and divine nature, have been clearly seen, being understood through what has been made, so that they are without excuse. For even though they knew God, they did not honor Him as God, or give thanks; but they became futile in their speculations, and their foolish heart was darkened. Professing to be wise, they became fools, and exchanged the glory of the incorruptible God for an image in the form of corruptible man and of birds and four-footed animals and crawling creatures. Therefore God gave them over in the lusts of their hearts to impurity, that their bodies might be dishonored among them" (vv. 19-24, NASB). Notice also verse 26: "For this reason God gave them over to degrading passions" (NASB). It is a solemn matter to set one's will against Almighty God.

Pharaoh's Progressive Resistance

The verses that refer to the hardening of Pharaoh's heart indicate a progressive hardening. These verses also reveal when and how God intervened.

As we have indicated, the key to the hardening of Pharaoh's heart is found in Exodus 5:2, which records his response to the command to let the people go: "Pharaoh said, Who is the Lord, that I should obey his voice to let Israel go? I know not the Lord, neither will I let Israel go."

Then, notice especially what the Lord told Moses in Exodus 6:1: "Now you shall see what I will do to Pharaoh; for under compulsion he shall let them go, and under compulsion he shall drive them out of his land" (NASB).

God announced to Moses that He would harden Pharaoh's heart and perform signs and wonders in order to

persuade Pharaoh and Egypt that God was who He said He
was. God told Moses, "But I will harden Pharaoh's heart that
I may multiply My signs and My wonders in the land of
Egypt. When Pharaoh will not listen to you, then I will lay
My hand on Egypt, and bring out My hosts, My people the
sons of Israel, from the land of Egypt by great judgments.
And the Egyptians shall know that I am the Lord, when I
stretch out My hand on Egypt and bring out the sons of
Israel from their midst" (7:3-5, NASB).

When would God harden Pharaoh's heart? Not until
Pharaoh had hardened his own heart and absolutely refused
to listen to Moses, God's representative. Aaron's first miracle
before Pharaoh was the throwing down of his rod, which
became a serpent. However, when Pharaoh called his wise
men and they were able to perform a similar miracle, this
caused Pharaoh's heart to be hardened and his mind to
become more stubborn. When his magicians were able to
duplicate the miracle, he apparently thought, "That shows
that my god is just as strong and powerful as your God, so
I'm not going to listen to you." It seemed to make no
difference to Pharaoh that Aaron's rod-turned-serpent
swallowed up those of the magicians. The Bible says, "Yet
Pharaoh's heart was hardened, and he did not listen to them,
as the Lord had said. Then the Lord said to Moses, 'Pharaoh's
heart is stubborn; he refuses to let the people go'" (7:13,14,
NASB).

Then followed several judgments, or plagues. After each
one of these judgments, the hardening of Pharaoh's heart is
emphasized. The obstinacy of his mind is seen in what the
Bible has to say about him. After Aaron caused the water to
turn into blood, the Bible says, "The magicians of Egypt did
the same with their secret arts; and Pharaoh's heart was
hardened, and he did not listen to them, as the Lord had
said" (v. 22, NASB).

But even later when the magicians could not duplicate
the miracles of Moses and Aaron, Pharaoh still refused to
heed God's command; his mind was rigidly set. This is
evident from Exodus 8:19: "Then the magicians said to
Pharaoh, 'This is the finger of God.' But Pharaoh's heart was
hardened, and he did not listen to them, as the Lord had
said" (NASB).

Even when Pharaoh realized that the judgments were falling only on the Egyptians and not on the Israelites, his heart still remained firmly fixed against God. Exodus 8 concludes by saying, "Pharaoh hardened his heart at this time also, neither would he let the people go" (v. 32). Even after these awful plagues, Pharaoh's heart was hardened—it was firmly fixed, insensitive to the voice of God and unaffected by the miracles that were performed before him.

Even though God had told Moses that He would harden Pharaoh's heart, the first mention of God actually doing this is in Exodus 9:12: "The Lord hardened the heart of Pharaoh, and he hearkened not unto them; as the Lord had spoken unto Moses." As to the time this took place, the account involved indicates that it was during the sixth judgment God brought on Pharaoh and the Egyptians. The words "the Lord hardened the heart of Pharaoh" could be literally translated, "Jehovah made the heart of Pharaoh firm." God simply confirmed that which was already hardened.

Pharaoh's Insincere Confessions

Moses had warned Pharaoh not to persist in his hardness. Earlier, during the fourth plague, Moses had told Pharaoh, "Behold, I go out from thee, and I will intreat the Lord that the swarms of flies may depart from Pharaoh, from his servants, and from his people, to morrow: but let not Pharaoh deal deceitfully any more in not letting the people go to sacrifice to the Lord" (Ex. 8:29).

Note also what the Lord told Moses to say to Pharaoh: "Thus speaks the Lord God of the Hebrews, Let My people go, so they may serve Me; for if you refuse to let them go and persist in detaining them, beware! The Lord's hand will be on your livestock out in the field, on the horses, the donkeys, the camels, the herds and the flocks with a dreadful plague. The Lord will draw distinction between Israel's livestock and that of Egypt. Nothing that belongs to the Israelites shall die" (9:1-4, Berkeley).

Exodus 9:16 is a key statement revealing God's purpose for hardening Pharaoh's heart and for keeping him alive rather than destroying him: "But for this very purpose have I let you live, that I might show you My power, and that My name may be declared throughout all the earth" (Amplified). This same thought is expressed in Romans 9:17: "For the scripture saith unto Pharaoh, Even for this same purpose have I raised thee up, that I might shew my power in thee, and that my name might be declared throughout all the earth."

God puts rulers on the throne, and He removes them from the throne. This is the responsibility and prerogative of the sovereign God. God was, in effect, saying to Pharaoh, "Pharaoh, I have allowed you to come to the throne, and I have allowed you to live so I can prove to Egypt and to My people that I am God Almighty—that I have all power."

As the result of the plagues which followed, Pharaoh began to weaken. He even confessed that he had sinned, although he said this only in an attempt to get Moses and Aaron to stop the plague. Pharaoh said, "I have sinned this time; the Lord is the righteous one, and I and my people are the wicked ones. Make supplication to the Lord, for there has been enough of God's thunder and hail; and I will let you go, and you shall stay no longer" (Ex. 9:27,28, NASB).

Moses agreed to pray that God would stop the plague, but he was not deceived by Pharaoh's false confession. Moses said, "But as for you and your servants, I know that you do not yet fear the Lord God" (v. 30, NASB). That God had given Moses correct insight into Pharaoh's heart is seen from verses 34 and 35: "But when Pharaoh saw that the rain and the hail and the thunder had ceased, he sinned again and hardened his heart, he and his servants. And Pharaoh's heart was hardened, and he did not let the sons of Israel go, just as the Lord had spoken through Moses" (NASB). It is obvious from this incident that Pharaoh himself, not God, hardened Pharaoh's heart.

The hardening of Pharaoh's heart is also mentioned in Exodus 10. The Lord told Moses, "Go to Pharaoh, for I have hardened his heart and the heart of his servants, that I may perform these signs of Mine among them, and that you may tell in the hearing of your son, and of your grandson, how I made a mockery of the Egyptians, and how I performed My signs among them; that you may know that I am the Lord" (vv. 1,2, NASB). Pharaoh attempted to mock God, but God made a mockery of Pharaoh and the Egyptians.

Pharaoh continued to resist God, but the Egyptians feared that the nation would be ruined by the plagues brought on them by Moses. "Pharaoh's servants said unto him, How long shall this man be a snare unto us? Let the men go, that they may serve the Lord their God: knowest thou not yet that Egypt is destroyed?" (v. 7).

But Pharaoh would not give in to the suggestions of his people, nor would he submit to God. A plague of locusts followed, and again Pharaoh feigned confession of sin in order to be relieved of the plague. "Pharaoh hurriedly called for Moses and Aaron, and he said, 'I have sinned against the Lord your God and against you. Now therefore, please forgive my sin only this once, and make supplication to the Lord your God, that He would only remove this death from me' " (vv. 16,17, NASB).

God Hardens Pharaoh's Heart

But Pharaoh was not sincere, and the Lord was not through with him: "The Lord hardened Pharaoh's heart, and he did not let the sons of Israel go" (v. 20, NASB). Verse 27 emphasizes the same truth: "But the Lord hardened Pharaoh's heart, and he was not willing to let them go" (NASB).

By this time, Pharaoh was really angry. He said to Moses, "Get away from me! Beware, do not see my face again, for in the day you see my face you shall die!" (v. 28, NASB). Upon hearing Pharaoh's words, Moses solemnly said to him, "You are right; I shall never see your face again!" (v. 29, NASB). But before Moses left Pharaoh's presence, Moses told him of the coming judgment on the firstborn of Egypt, and then he "went out from Pharaoh in hot anger" (11:8, NASB).

Then the Lord told Moses, "Pharaoh will not listen to you, that My wonders and miracles may be multiplied in the land of Egypt. Moses and Aaron did all these wonders and miracles before Pharaoh; and the Lord hardened Pharaoh's stubborn heart, and he did not let the Israelites go out of his land" (vv. 9,10, Amplified). Notice from these verses that God hardened Pharaoh's already stubborn heart.

After the firstborn of Egypt had been destroyed and the Israelites had fled, God told Moses, "I will harden Pharaoh's heart, that he shall follow after them; and I will be honoured upon Pharaoh, and upon all his host; that the Egyptians may know that I am the Lord. And they did so" (14:4). This was the final hardening of Pharaoh's heart. Verse 8 says, "The Lord hardened the heart of Pharaoh king of Egypt, and he pursued after the children of Israel: and the children of Israel went out with an high hand."

God not only hardened the heart of Pharaoh, but He also hardened the hearts of the Egyptians so that they pursued the Israelites to the Red Sea (vv. 17,18). But the Lord drowned the Egyptians in the Red Sea after the Israelites had crossed over on dry ground. "Thus the Lord saved Israel that day out of the hand of the Egyptians; and Israel saw the Egyptians dead upon the sea shore. And Israel saw that great work which the Lord did upon the Egyptians: and the people feared the Lord, and believed the Lord, and his servant Moses" (vv. 30,31). What a climax!

Remember that the hardening of Pharaoh's heart is ascribed both to Pharaoh and to God. It is not necessary or right to make God the author of Pharaoh's stubbornness. And God did not arbitrarily or directly force on Pharaoh an obstinate and stubborn resistance to Himself. God can never be blamed for evil.

From the Book of James we learn that God does not solicit or cause a person to do evil. When a person does evil, it is because of his own depraved nature. James said, "Let no man say when he is tempted, I am tempted of God: for God cannot be tempted with evil, neither tempteth he any man: but every man is tempted, when he is drawn away of his own lust, and enticed. Then when lust hath conceived, it bringeth forth sin: and sin, when it is finished, bringeth forth death. Do not err, my beloved brethren" (1:13-16).

As we have seen, God told Moses about the hardening of Pharaoh's heart even before the plagues began. Although man looks on the outer appearance, God looks on the heart—He is a heart specialist!

During the first five plagues Pharaoh hardened his own heart. It was only after the sixth plague that God finally confirmed Pharaoh in his hardness. The extent to which

Pharaoh had hardened his own heart is seen in Exodus 5:2—he refused to acknowledge God or to do what He said.

During the last five plagues Pharaoh not only hardened his own heart, but God also confirmed Pharaoh in that hardness. Even after the magicians of Egypt were unable to duplicate the miracles of Moses and Aaron and admitted that the miracles were from God (8:19), Pharaoh still refused to submit to God.

Important Lessons for Today

It is dangerous for a person to know the truth and to deliberately sin against that knowledge. Pharaoh would not bend his will to the will of God, regardless of the power manifested by God.

From the hardening of Pharaoh's heart, we can learn some important lessons. First, God never allows any person to continue to scoff at Him. The Bible emphasizes this truth in Galatians 6:7: "Be not deceived; God is not mocked: for whatsoever a man soweth, that shall he also reap."

Second, God not only permits man to harden himself, but—after being patient and longsuffering—He also produces a stubbornly resistant and unyielding heart attitude in that person.

Third, for a time God withholds, or postpones, judgment on the person who hardens his heart against Him. These three facts are seen throughout the account of Exodus, and they are important principles for us to keep in mind.

The curse of sin makes the heart hardened toward God. At first God permits this stubbornness to be manifested toward Him, but eventually He confirms a person in that hardness and thus deliberately hardens the person's heart. The sinner's heart can become so stubbornly unyielding that it is no longer capable of turning from its fixed position against God. Thus, the sinner is brought into the judgment of damnation.

Perhaps someone reading these lines has resisted God just as Pharaoh did. If so, do you realize that your heart can become so hard that you may never again have a desire to turn to God?

Although God gave him opportunity again and again to repent, Pharaoh was so hardened in his ways that he refused to change his mind concerning God and his own need of salvation. After his heart was firmly fixed in its hardness, God then confirmed it so that Pharaoh never again had a desire to turn to God. As we have seen, Pharaoh's admission of being a sinner was not sincere at all but was only an attempt to stop whatever plague he was experiencing.

After the seventh plague Pharaoh's heart was so hard that judgment was the only course left to God. And with the judgment of God upon him, Pharaoh's heart was completely hardened by God. As a result, Pharaoh and his army pursued the Israelites and were overtaken by God's final stroke of judgment in the Red Sea. God's hardening of Pharaoh's heart only completed what Pharaoh had already done to his own heart.

This should remove every reason for questioning what God did. We are compelled to see that God left Pharaoh's heart in its natural state; that is, obstinate, inflexible and full of iniquity. God had a perfect right to allow Pharaoh to continue in a disobedient, God-defying attitude. Pharaoh had refused to obey God or to acknowledge Him in any way. In God's infinite wisdom and knowledge, He read with unerring accuracy what was in Pharaoh's heart, and He was completely justified in confirming Pharaoh in his hardness.

God knows your heart too. He knows whether or not you are full of stubbornness. God may allow you to go your own way until He finally has to bring some type of judgment on you. If you have trusted Jesus Christ as your personal Saviour, God's judgment will not be eternal damnation, but He could severely chasten you to bring you back into fellowship with Himself. But when death comes, there is no other opportunity for those who refuse to trust Jesus Christ as Saviour to be saved. The Bible says, "It is appointed unto men once to die, but after this the judgment" (Heb. 9:27).

New Testament Commentary

In considering what God has said about the hardening of Pharaoh's heart, we should give attention to a key New Testament passage on this subject. Romans 9 is frequently cited in explaining what was involved in the hardening of Pharaoh's heart. Yet even Romans 9 has been interpreted in different ways. We want to examine this passage, for it is the New Testament commentary on this Old Testament event.

"For the scripture saith unto Pharaoh, Even for this same purpose have I raised thee up, that I might shew my power in thee, and that my name might be declared throughout all the earth. . . . What if God, willing to shew his wrath, and to make his power known, endured with much longsuffering the vessels of wrath fitted to destruction: and that he might make known the riches of his glory on the vessels of mercy, which he had afore prepared unto glory" (vv. 17,22,23).

God resolved to use Pharaoh as an example of His sovereignty because Pharaoh was incorrigible—he was incapable of being corrected, for he was unalterably depraved. God simply used Pharaoh as He found him to demonstrate His power to the human race, an act of perfect justice to Pharaoh because all of God's demands were just.

The words "for this same purpose have I raised thee up" (v. 17) have caused many to stumble in their interpretation. These words do not mean that God created Pharaoh for the purpose of using him as a demonstration of damnation. Rather, they refer to God allowing Pharaoh to appear, or to be brought forward on the stage of events. God had a purpose to fulfill, and Pharaoh was the right person to be on the throne at that time in order for God to fulfill His purpose. That God is even in control of earthly powers is seen in Daniel 4:17: "This matter is by the decree of the watchers, and the demand by the word of the holy ones: to the intent that the living may know that the most High ruleth in the kingdom of men, and giveth it to whomsoever he will, and setteth up over it the basest of men." God has the right to place on the throne the person of His choice.

The significance of Romans 9:17 is that God allowed Pharaoh to be on the throne so that He could demonstrate His power.

Romans 9:22 is the first part of a long question in which Paul asked, "What if God, willing to shew his wrath, and to make his power known, endured with much longsuffering the vessels of wrath fitted to destruction?" Please note that God "endured with much longsuffering" and also that the vessels

under discussion were those "fitted to destruction."
Although God's righteous nature eventually led Him to
demonstrate His wrath against evil, He withheld His wrath
and endured patiently for a long time.

So we see that God had every right to destroy Pharaoh
and all of Egypt much earlier than He did. When Pharaoh
refused to obey or to even recognize Him (Ex. 5:2) and
called God's words vain babblings (v. 9), God would have
been completely justified in destroying Pharaoh and his
people with a bolt of fire from heaven. But God held
back—He endured with longsuffering, and in so doing He gave
the entire world a demonstration of how He could be
merciful, even to a blasphemer such as Pharaoh. But God's
power and wrath were also revealed to the world when God
accomplished His will through Pharaoh and finally brought
judgment on him. God had every right to allow Pharaoh to
continue in his disobedient, God-defying attitude and also to
bring judgment on him at once.

Notice particularly the last words of Romans 9:22: "The
vessels of wrath fitted to destruction." These are significant
words. God did not fit the vessels for wrath nor were they
fitted by God for destruction. The word "fitted" is not
equivalent to "foreordained" or "foreknown." Rather, these
vessels were fitted in the sense that they were ready, or ripe,
for destruction. It was evident from what Pharaoh said and
did that he was fully ready for judgment.

In our study of the first five plagues that God brought on
Pharaoh and the Egyptians, we have seen that God did not
touch Pharaoh himself; God allowed him to go on in his own
destructive way. Even though Pharaoh said he did not know
God and made it clear that he did not intend to listen to
God, he was still spared from destruction in the first five
plagues. This reveals that Pharaoh hardened his heart in spite
of the fact that God was longsuffering and merciful to him.
God sent a plague, and then through Moses He took it away,
thereby giving Pharaoh every opportunity to repent. But he
absolutely refused. Because of his rejection of God's grace in
the first five plagues, God then further hardened, or
confirmed, Pharaoh's hardened heart in the sixth plague.

It is not always the judgment of God that brings people
to repentance. God was showing His mercy to Pharaoh, and

this was in line with the principle stated in Romans 2:4-6: "Or do you think lightly of the riches of His kindness and forbearance and patience, not knowing that the kindness of God leads you to repentance? But because of your stubbornness and unrepentant heart you are storing up wrath for yourself in the day of wrath and revelation of the righteous judgment of God; who will render to every man according to his deeds" (NASB).

Notice also the significant statement made in II Peter 3:15: "And account that the longsuffering of our Lord is salvation."

Although God gave Pharaoh and the Egyptians every opportunity to repent and to turn to Him for salvation, they refused to do so. In refusing the mercy and longsuffering of God, they became vessels fitted to, or ready for, destruction.

God's Mercy and God's Judgment

God's dealings with Pharaoh and the Egyptians teach a valuable lesson to everyone today. God also expresses His mercy and longsuffering to sinners now, but He will not withhold His judgment forever. So one should not delay in trusting Christ as Saviour. As II Corinthians 6:2 says, "Behold, now is 'the acceptable time,' behold, now is 'the day of salvation' " (NASB).

There are many indications that God is withholding His wrath against sin today. He allows blasphemous people to go unhindered in what they are saying. There seems to be a drive to eliminate any reference to God in the classrooms of North America. At the same time, many are aggressively seeking to expose students to all kinds of filthy literature. In His longsuffering, God is allowing people to speak blasphemous words against Him, but He will not always withhold judgment. We must never forget that a day of judgment is coming.

God is withholding His wrath today so that He can reveal His mercy and glory to those who will accept His gift of salvation. We must remember that people are not lost because they are hardened; they are hardened because they are lost. And the reason for their lost condition is that all are born into this world with a sinful nature. "All have sinned, and come short of the glory of God" (Rom. 3:23).

So the hardening of Pharaoh's heart was the fruit of his sin. It was the result of his self-will, high-mindedness and pride, all of which result from sin. Pharaoh continued to abuse the freedom of the will which is present in every man and which makes it possible to remain obstinate and to resist the Word of God. When one continues to reject God's love, he will eventually experience God's judgment.

A sinner may resist the will of God as long as he lives, but such resistance plunges him into destruction and damnation at death. God never allows a person to scoff at Him without eventually experiencing judgment unless that person repents. Pharaoh scoffed at God, and God waited for some time without bringing destruction on him, but destruction finally came. After Pharaoh had hardened his heart against God, he was then used by God as a further demonstration of God's power.

The Bible alludes many times to the serious responsibility we have before God. To the Jews, Christ said, "Ye will not come to me, that ye might have life" (John 5:40). Stephen said to the same people, "Ye stiffnecked and uncircumcised in heart and ears, ye do always resist the Holy Ghost: as your fathers did, so do ye" (Acts 7:51). Solomon said, "He, that being often reproved hardeneth his neck, shall suddenly be destroyed, and that without remedy" (Prov. 29:1).

God's Desire for All Men

But Peter said, "The Lord is not slack concerning his promise, as some men count slackness; but is longsuffering to us-ward, not willing that any should perish, but that all should come to repentance" (II Pet. 3:9). God does not want to see people die in their sins; He "desires all men to be saved and to come to the knowledge of the truth" (I Tim. 2:4, NASB).

Through Ezekiel, God said, "I have no pleasure in the death of the wicked; but that the wicked turn from his way and live: turn ye, turn ye from your evil ways; for why will ye die, O house of Israel?" (Ezek. 33:11). The Book of Hebrews warns, "Wherefore (as the Holy Ghost saith, To day if ye will hear his voice, harden not your hearts, as in the provocation, in the day of temptation in the wilderness.) . . . Take heed, brethren, lest there be in any of you an evil heart of unbelief, in departing from the living God" (3:7,8,12).

Romans 2:4,5 says, "Or despisest thou the riches of his goodness and forbearance and longsuffering; not knowing that the goodness of God leadeth thee to repentance? But after thy hardness and impenitent heart treasurest up unto thyself wrath against the day of wrath and revelation of the righteous judgment of God." Thus, Galatians 6:7,8 warns, "Be not deceived; God is not mocked: for whatsoever a man soweth, that shall he also reap. For he that soweth to his flesh shall of the flesh reap corruption; but he that soweth to the Spirit shall of the Spirit reap life everlasting."

It is important that each person take these warnings from the Word of God seriously. But notice also the invitation that Christ extends to us: "Come unto me, all ye that labour and are heavy laden, and I will give you rest. Take my yoke upon you, and learn of me; for I am meek and lowly in heart: and ye shall find rest unto your souls. For my yoke is easy, and my burden is light" (Matt. 11:28-30). The Lord Jesus Christ also promised, "All that the Father giveth me shall come to me; and him that cometh to me I will in no wise cast out" (John 6:37). Have you trusted Jesus Christ as your personal Saviour? If not, do so today before it is eternally too late.

Chapter 6

The Progressive Intensity of the Plagues

There is an evident progression in the intensity of the ten plagues. Because the tenth plague—the killing of the firstborn—is worthy of special attention in itself, in this chapter we want to focus attention on the first nine. Only because Pharaoh refused to be influenced by the first nine plagues was the tenth severe judgment brought by God. However, God—in His omniscience—announced the tenth plague even at the beginning (Ex. 4:22,23).

As previously discussed, God had at least four purposes for bringing the plagues on Pharaoh and the Egyptians. First, they revealed God's mighty power, showing that He was greater than any of the gods of Egypt. The Egyptians were so entrenched in idol worship that the true God had to perform miracles to show who He was. Second, the plagues were to break Pharaoh's stubbornness so he would let the Israelites go. This was not accomplished, however, until the very end. Third, the plagues were to strengthen Moses' faith. He needed this strengthening as preparation for the years when he would be Israel's leader in the desert. Fourth, the plagues were meant to soften the hearts of the Israelites and cause them to want to leave Egypt. Even though life was difficult for the Israelites in Egypt, they were unwilling to leave at first. But the plagues made them willing to go.

Although skeptics often look at the account of the plagues and claim that they were only natural phenomena that had occurred periodically in a lighter form over Egypt, there are several reasons why this is not a valid view. God caused the people of that day to realize He was doing something on a special scale that was incomparable to anything else. The plagues were brought on the country and then removed like clockwork, according to Moses' announcements. They came when he said they would come, and they stopped when he said they would stop.

The plagues revealed the protective power of God as He shielded His people. They also demonstrated the omnipotence of the true God and the impotence of the Egyptian gods. Although, under the power of Satan, the Egyptian magicians could imitate some of the miracles, they could not imitate all of them.

Then, too, the intensity of the plagues was something that had never been experienced before and will not be experienced again until God speaks during the coming Tribulation. If Pharaoh and the Egyptians were not convinced that the plagues were more than natural phenomena, they would never have allowed the Israelites to leave Egypt. But Pharaoh and the Egyptians were not only willing to let the Israelites go, they even drove them out of the country.

Before the plagues came on Egypt, God announced to Moses what He was about to do: "I am aware that the king of Egypt will not allow you to go except by a mighty hand, so I will stretch out My hand and strike Egypt with all the wonders I shall work there; after which he will send you away. And I will give this people such favor with the Egyptians that when you leave, you will not go empty-handed; but each woman shall request from her neighbor and from the lodger in her home silver and gold articles, and garments with which you will dress your sons and daughters. You shall strip the Egyptians" (Ex. 3:19-22, Berkeley).

We have discussed previously how Moses and Aaron obeyed God's instructions down to the last detail because they believed God. "Moses and Aaron did as the Lord ordered them, to the last syllable" (7:6, Berkeley). Thus faith and obedience were the keys to their success; Moses and Aaron did absolutely everything the Lord told them to do.

Moses and Aaron first went before Pharaoh and presented their credentials—Aaron's rod became a serpent right before Pharaoh's eyes! But then Pharaoh called his wise men and they "did the same by their secret formulas" (v. 11,

Berkeley). But Aaron's credentials were proven superior when his staff swallowed the others. Although Pharaoh did not accept the message of Moses and Aaron at this time, he had to deal with them as men of authority. The fact that Aaron's snake swallowed up the snakes of the Egyptian magicians revealed God's power over the gods of Egypt.

Moses' faith is seen throughout the process and progress of the plagues. Hebrews 11:27 gives credit to Moses in these words: "By faith he forsook Egypt, not fearing the wrath of the king: for he endured, as seeing him who is invisible." By faith he forsook Egypt and by faith he endured, because he saw the invisible God. Moses' faith grew; it was strengthened through the tests he faced and by the plagues on Egypt so that he saw and understood God more clearly.

Moses' faith was the means, or the instrument, by which God worked His mighty wonders on Egypt. Although God is almighty and, therefore, can do anything, He often chooses to express His power primarily through individuals. But God requires that the individuals have complete faith in Him. Thus, Moses' faith was the means by which God conducted great miracles on the earth.

Even though Moses and Aaron had miraculous credentials, Pharaoh refused to heed what they had to say. God then gave Moses and Aaron these instructions: "In the morning, when as usual he is going out to the water, stand by the river bank to meet him. Take in your hand the staff that became a snake and say to him, 'The Lord God of the Hebrews has sent me to you with the message: "Let My people go, so they may serve Me in the desert." But to date you have not listened' " (Ex. 7:15,16, Berkeley).

The First Plague

God then instructed Moses to tell Aaron to stretch his staff over the waters of Egypt "so they shall become blood in the whole country of Egypt, the contents of wooden and stone containers included" (v. 19, Berkeley).

The plague came about precisely as God had foretold. The rivers, especially the Nile, were affected along with all canals. All water was turned into blood. For seven full days this condition prevailed. Fish died and floated to the surface; the air reeked with corruption. There was no water to drink in the land, so the Egyptians had to dig near the riverbank for water (v. 24). Notice that the Egyptian wise men were able to imitate this same miracle by their secret formulas (v. 22).

The Egyptians worshiped the Nile, but the goddess of the Nile could do nothing about this plague. God Almighty was far greater than the sacred Nile. So this miracle struck directly at the gods of Egypt so that all would know the absolute power of the true God.

The Second Plague

Because Pharaoh refused to let the people go, a second plague was brought on him and the Egyptians.

"The Lord spake unto Moses, Go unto Pharaoh, and say unto him, Thus saith the Lord, Let my people go, that they may serve me" (Ex. 8:1).

God warned what the plague would be if Pharaoh refused: "If thou refuse to let them go, behold, I will smite all thy borders with frogs: and the river shall bring forth frogs abundantly, which shall go up and come into thine house, and into thy bedchamber, and upon thy bed, and into the house of thy servants, and upon thy people, and into thine ovens, and into thy kneading-troughs: and the frogs shall come up both on thee, and upon thy people, and upon all thy servants" (vv. 2-4).

Notice that God gave Pharaoh another chance to repent, inasmuch as He announced the plague in advance. The plague was to come on Pharaoh and the Egyptians only if Pharaoh refused to let the Israelites go. Because Pharaoh refused, "the Lord spake unto Moses, Say unto Aaron, Stretch forth thine hand with thy rod over the streams, over the rivers, and over the ponds, and cause frogs to come up upon the land of Egypt" (v. 5).

It is significant that this second plague involved frogs, because frogs were also an object of worship in Egypt. Again, the true God showed His superiority over the gods of Egypt. Because the frog was worshiped, it was sacrilegious for an Egyptian to attempt to destroy it. This fact made the plague especially horrible on the Egyptians.

But again, the magicians of Egypt were not to be outdone
by Moses and Aaron. Verse 7 says that the magicians "did the
same with their secret formulas; they brought up frogs on the
Egyptian country" (Berkeley). How interesting—the
Egyptians certainly did not need more frogs! Yet, while the
magicians were able to imitate the miracle of producing frogs,
they were unable to bring an end to this plague.

Pharaoh seemingly began to weaken, for he "called for
Moses and Aaron, and said, Intreat the Lord, that he may
take away the frogs from me, and from my people; and I will
let the people go, that they may do sacrifice unto the Lord"
(v. 8).

To make the supremacy and power of God more obvious,
Moses said to him, "Glory over me: when shall I intreat for
thee, and for thy servants, and for thy people, to destroy the
frogs from thee and thy houses, that they may remain in the
river only?" (v. 9). "Glory over me" implies "the honor is
yours to tell me." All Pharaoh had to do was say the word to
Moses and the plague would be stopped. In answer to Moses'
question, Pharaoh replied, "To morrow" (v. 10). Moses
agreed, for he said, "Be it according to thy word: that thou
mayest know that there is none like unto the Lord our God"
(v. 10). Notice again that the only one who could stop the
plague was Moses, God's representative. The magicians of
Egypt could not stop it. They, like Satan whom they served,
could originate evil, but they could not stop its progress.

Faithful to his word, "Moses cried unto the Lord because
of the frogs which he had brought against Pharaoh. And the
Lord did according to the word of Moses; and the frogs died
out of the houses, out of the villages, and out of the fields"
(vv. 12,13). The ending of this plague was a miracle just as
producing the frogs had been a miracle.

But think of what a mess all the dead frogs caused! "The
people piled them in heaps till the land reeked" (v. 14,
Berkeley). What was Pharaoh's response after the plague was
ended? Verse 15 gives the answer: "But when Pharaoh
noticed that relief had come, he stiffened his heart; he did
not heed them, as the Lord had said" (Berkeley). Pharaoh
hardened his heart again!

The Third Plague

Because of the further hardening of Pharaoh's heart, another plague was brought on him and the Egyptians. There is no indication that Pharaoh was forewarned of this third plague; the hardening of his heart after the second plague was reason enough for God to bring another judgment.

"The Lord said unto Moses, Say unto Aaron, Stretch out thy rod, and smite the dust of the land, that it may become lice throughout all the land of Egypt" (v. 16). Imagine what this terrible plague must have been like—millions of lice! But these judgments were coming on Pharaoh because he had refused to obey God or to even recognize Him (5:2).

The magicians of Egypt also attempted to imitate this third plague but were unable to do so (8:18). By imitating the plagues, the Egyptian magicians were attempting to show that the god they served (Satan) was as great as the God that Moses and Aaron served. However, they were able to do only what God allowed them to do. He had allowed them to imitate the previous miracles but not this one. This immediately brought consternation to the magicians, and they said to Pharaoh, "This is the finger of God" (v. 19). When God no longer permitted the magicians to duplicate miracles, the magicians were powerless, regardless of how hard they tried. This caused them to realize that the miracle Aaron had performed was truly of God.

The magicians were deriving their power from Satan, and from Job 1 and 2 we learn that Satan can only do what God allows him to do. Hebrews 2:14 tells how the Lord Jesus Christ broke the power of Satan: "Since then the children share in flesh and blood, He Himself likewise also partook of the same, that through death He might render powerless him who had the power of death, that is, the devil" (NASB). Satan's bounds are prescribed by God.

The plague of lice particularly vexed the Egyptians because they were scrupulously clean in their personal habits. This was especially true of the Egyptian priests. Although serving false gods, the Egyptian priests would repeatedly bathe and shave themselves in preparation for their sacred duties.

Also, since some of the animals were worshiped—such as the bulls and goats—they were kept very clean, but they also became infected with lice. No Egyptian man or animal was spared—there were lice on men and beasts (Ex. 8:17). Thus, God again executed judgment on the gods of Egypt so all would know that He was the true God.

Even though the Egyptian magicians told Pharaoh, "This is the finger of God" (v. 19), Pharaoh would not pay any attention to their words; his heart became all the harder. The magicians were convinced that this plague was the result of a much higher power than they knew about. However, there is no indication that the magicians voiced their opinion to Pharaoh more than once.

God exalted Himself above the gods of Egypt, and Philippians 2 tells us that Jesus Christ has been exalted above every name because He became obedient to death on the cross: "Wherefore God also hath highly exalted him, and given him a name which is above every name: that at the name of Jesus every knee should bow, of things in heaven, and things in earth, and things under the earth; and that every tongue should confess that Jesus Christ is Lord, to the glory of God the Father" (vv. 9-11). This passage is comparable to Isaiah 45:23: "I have sworn by myself, the word is gone out of my mouth in righteousness, and shall not return, That unto me every knee shall bow, every tongue shall swear."

These first three plagues which came on Pharaoh and the Egyptians were directed specifically at their comfort and cleanliness, and the Israelites as well as the Egyptians suffered from them. As Pharaoh became harder and harder, Israel was made to see that God was working in their behalf. This became more apparent later, as the plagues came only on the Egyptians, and the Israelites were spared. God allowed Satan to go just so far and no further as far as touching His own. The Israelites were subject to the basic influences of sin, but later, when God dealt out destruction on property and lives, the Israelites were spared.

The Fourth Plague

The first nine plagues can be grouped into three series, each consisting of three plagues. Therefore, the fourth plague began a new series. In the next three plagues God brought destruction on the property and lives of the Egyptians but spared Israel.

The fourth plague is recorded in Exodus 8:20-32. The magicians and their gods had been proven to be fakes, so they could not oppose the rest of the plagues. They had succumbed to the powers of the Almighty God. Satan and his demons were not able to imitate or withstand the plague God was about to bring on Pharaoh and the Egyptians.

The Lord told Moses, "Rise up early in the morning, and stand before Pharaoh; lo, he cometh forth to the water; and say unto him, Thus saith the Lord, Let my people go, that they may serve me. Else, if thou wilt not let my people go, behold, I will send swarms of flies upon thee, and upon thy servants, and upon thy people, and into thy houses: and the houses of the Egyptians shall be full of swarms of flies, and also the ground whereon they are" (vv. 20,21). Notice that God gave Pharaoh another opportunity to repent before He brought this plague. But, as happened previously, Pharaoh refused to repent and only further hardened his own heart against the Lord.

This plague involved "swarms of flies" (v. 21). In the King James Version the word "flies" is italicized, meaning there is no basis for the word in the original language but that it was added by the translators to assist the meaning. The original says only that there were swarms; what they were swarms of is not exactly specified. It may have been flies, as the King James translators indicated, but there are also other possibilities. The Berkeley Version says "gadflies," and the New American Standard Bible says "insects." It is probably best to understand these swarms as a mixture of all kinds of flies. Later, when the psalmist wrote of this plague, he referred to "divers sorts of flies" (Ps. 78:45).

Among these insects may well have been the particular beetle that was the emblem of the Egyptian sun god. If so, this plague was another demonstration of the power of the true God over the false gods of Egypt.

In announcing the fourth plague to Pharaoh, God said through Moses, "I will sever in that day the land of Goshen, in which my people dwell, that no swarms of flies shall be there; to the end thou mayest know that I am the Lord in the midst of the earth. And I will put a division between my people and thy people: to morrow shall this sign be" (Ex. 8:22,23).

The lice had previously brought much discomfort to the Egyptians, but that was nothing in comparison to the discomfort resulting from the swarms of insects because they actually fed on the flesh of the people. This is indicated by Psalm 78:45: "He sent divers sorts of flies among them, which devoured them." Thus, the swarms of insects directly affected human flesh as well as vegetation.

Consider the great contrast between the Israelites and the Egyptians. The Israelites were only slaves of the Egyptians, but the God of the slaves completely overcame the gods of their masters. The God of Israel brought judgment on the Egyptians, yet the Israelites were completely protected. What a God!

All of this was too much for Pharaoh, and again he weakened under the tremendous pressure. He finally granted permission for the Israelites to leave, but his permission included restrictions that tested Moses' willingness to compromise. The Bible says, "Then Pharaoh called for Moses and Aaron and said, 'You go and sacrifice to your God within our boundaries' " (Ex. 8:25, Berkeley). Pharaoh was not yet willing to let the Israelites completely leave the land of Egypt.

But notice Moses' response: "It would not be right to do that; for we would offer the Lord our God something offensive to the Egyptians. You see, if we offer something the Egyptians abominate right before their eyes, might they not stone us? We want to go three days' travel into the desert to sacrifice to the Lord our God the way He directs us" (vv. 26,27, Berkeley).

Moses took a firm stand against the offer of Pharaoh. In particular, he pointed out that the Israelites' sacrifices would be considered an abomination by the Egyptians. Moses probably referred not only to the method of sacrificing but also to the animals sacrificed. The Egyptians considered various animals to be sacred, and they would be outraged if they saw the Israelites sacrificing these animals.

Pharaoh yielded to Moses' reasoning on this matter and then offered a second compromise: "I will let you go, that ye may sacrifice to the Lord your God in the wilderness; only ye shall not go very far away: intreat for me" (v. 28). Pharaoh was asking Moses to pray for him, while at the same time laying down restrictions about the Israelites' leaving Egypt.

Moses responded, "Behold, I go out from thee, and I will intreat the Lord that the swarms of flies may depart from Pharaoh, from his servants, and from his people, to morrow: but let not Pharaoh deal deceitfully any more in not letting the people go to sacrifice to the Lord" (v. 29). Moses boldly warned Pharaoh not to change his mind as he had done previously. But in spite of Moses' warning, after the swarms of insects were removed from Pharaoh and his people, "Pharaoh hardened his heart at this time also, neither would he let the people go" (v. 32). The Berkeley Version says, "Pharaoh set his mind stubbornly; he did not let the people go."

The Fifth Plague

Pharaoh's belligerent attitude resulted in the fifth plague, which is referred to in Exodus 9:1-7. The Lord told Moses, "Call on Pharaoh and tell him, 'Thus speaks the Lord God of the Hebrews, Let My people go, so they may serve Me; for if you refuse to let them go and persist in detaining them, beware! The Lord's hand will be on your livestock out in the field, on the horses, the donkeys, the camels, the herds and the flocks with a dreadful plague. The Lord will draw distinction between Israel's livestock and that of Egypt. Nothing that belongs to the Israelites shall die' " (vv. 1-4, Berkeley).

God again gave Pharaoh fair warning with an opportunity to obey, but again Pharaoh only further hardened his heart. This plague struck at the possessions of Pharaoh and the Egyptians, and next to health, this is what man values the most. But while this plague came on the livestock of Egypt, the livestock of Israel were unharmed.

By announcing that the plague would not begin until the next day, God gave Pharaoh 24 hours to repent. But since Pharaoh did not repent, God brought the plague precisely as He had announced.

Imagine the effect that the serious disease had on the Egyptian's animals. Egypt's sacred cows would have been dying everywhere, but in Israel the cattle would have been totally unaffected. Among the Egyptians there would have been death of livestock among the wealthy as well as among the poor. The horses of the rich died; donkeys of the poor died; camels that carried their merchandise to foreign countries died; oxen that plowed the fields died; sheep that constituted the great portion of Egyptian wealth died. The land was everywhere filled with death. Many are going bankrupt today, and unemployment is high, but imagine what it was like in that day due to the tremendous losses suffered by the Egyptians.

As this plague became so awful among the Egyptians, Pharaoh had an investigation made to see whether or not the Israelites in Goshen were affected. Exodus 9:7 says, "Pharaoh sent to investigate and found that not one of the Israelites' animals was dead; yet Pharaoh's mind was set; he did not let the people go" (Berkeley). This reveals how hard Pharaoh's heart really was; even after proof that this was obviously of God, he refused to humble himself before God. This was deliberate sinning against better knowledge. Again and again God had given him opportunity to repent, but Pharaoh only became more rebellious toward God.

Pharaoh was now ready for God's final judgment, but true to His character, God still extended mercy to Pharaoh. This especially reminds us of Romans 9:22: "What if God, willing to shew his wrath, and to make his power known, endured with much longsuffering the vessels of wrath fitted to destruction."

The Sixth Plague

Because of the hardness of Pharaoh's heart, another plague was brought on him and the Egyptians. Since Pharaoh's heart was incurably hardened, the Bible speaks from this point on of God's hardening Pharaoh's heart.

God told Moses and Aaron, "Both of you fill your hands with ashes from the furnace and, with Pharaoh looking on, let Moses toss it up to the sky. It will turn to fine dust all over the land of Egypt, that settles upon man and beast and causes boils that break out in open sores" (Ex. 9:8,9, Berkeley).

They did precisely as the Lord instructed, and all people and animals in Egypt were affected. Verse 11 says, "The scribes could not stand before Moses because of the sores: for the scribes as well as the rest of the Egyptians were covered with sores" (Berkeley). We then read this significant statement: "And the Lord hardened the heart of Pharaoh, and he hearkened not unto them; as the Lord had spoken unto Moses" (v. 12). Because Pharaoh had hardened his own heart against God so many times, he became one of the "vessels of wrath fitted to destruction" (Rom. 9:22); God hardened his heart.

God instructed Moses, "Rise up early in the morning, and stand before Pharaoh, and say unto him, Thus saith the Lord God of the Hebrews, Let my people go, that they may serve me. For I will at this time send all my plagues upon thine heart, and upon thy servants, and upon thy people; that thou mayest know that there is none like me in all the earth. For now I will stretch out my hand, that I may smite thee and thy people with pestilence; and thou shalt be cut off from the earth. And in very deed for this cause have I raised thee up, for to shew in thee my power; and that my name may be declared throughout all the earth" (Ex. 9:13-16).

The King James Version gives the impression that God created Pharaoh just to show His power and majesty. However, notice how the same verses are translated in another version: "Then the Lord said to Moses, Rise up early in the morning and stand before Pharaoh and say to him, Thus says the Lord, the God of the Hebrews, Let My people go, that they may serve Me. For this time I will send all My plagues upon your heart, and upon your servants and your people, that you may recognize and know that there is none like Me in all the earth.

"For by now I could have put forth My hand and have struck you and your people with pestilence, and you would have been cut off from the earth. But for this very purpose have I let you live, that I might show you My power, and that My name may be declared throughout all the earth" (Amplified).

Although Pharaoh was a vessel fitted for destruction, God exercised much longsuffering and patience in his behalf. God saw in Pharaoh a person who was obstinate to the point of rebelling against God Himself, yet God let him live so that the whole world would know that God was truly God. But we must remember that the longsuffering and mercy of God cannot continue to be scoffed at without suffering the consequences.

Pharaoh continued to oppose God and all that He stood for. Through Moses, God asked Pharaoh, "As yet exaltest thou thyself against my people, that thou wilt not let them go?" (v. 17). Because of Pharaoh's obstinacy, God brought another plague on him and the Egyptians.

The Seventh Plague

Because Pharaoh had refused to heed God in any way, God told Pharaoh through Moses, "Behold, to morrow about this time I will cause it to rain a very grievous hail, such as hath not been in Egypt since the foundation thereof even until now. Send therefore now, and gather thy cattle, and all that thou hast in the field; for upon every man and beast which shall be found in the field, and shall not be brought home, the hail shall come down upon them, and they shall die" (Ex. 9:18,19).

Notice that the Egyptians were acquainted with hailstorms, but this was to be a plague of hail such as the land had never experienced before. God said He would send the hail the next day, which gave Pharaoh another day of grace to submit to God and allow the Israelites to leave.

Although one day may seem to be a short time to consider this, remember that Pharaoh had already had days, weeks and months to consider the matter. So another entire day really was an abundant extension of God's grace. Pharaoh had deliberately hardened his own heart so many times that even this added day of grace made no impact on him. God's announcement of coming judgment fell on ears that refused to hear; Pharaoh's heart had become like clay hardened by the sun.

Notice, however, that some Egyptians responded to God's message of coming judgment: "He that feared the word of the Lord among the servants of Pharaoh made his servants and his cattle flee into the houses: and he that regarded not the word of the Lord left his servants and his cattle in the field" (vv. 20,21). These two verses reveal that a person's actions demonstrate whether or not he really believes God. Though some believed what God said, many others did not think that such a hailstorm would really come.

In accordance with God's instructions, "Moses stretched forth his rod toward heaven: and the Lord sent thunder and hail, and the fire ran along upon the ground; and the Lord rained hail upon the land of Egypt. So there was hail, and fire mingled with the hail, very grievous, such as there was none like it in all the land of Egypt since it became a nation. And the hail smote throughout all the land of Egypt all that was in the field, both man and beast; and the hail smote every herb of the field, and brake every tree of the field" (vv. 23-25).

But against the backdrop of this awful judgment is a verse that reveals God's protection of His own: "Only in the land of Goshen, where the children of Israel were, was there no hail" (v. 26). Goshen was part of Egypt, but God controlled the circumstances so that the Israelites were untouched by the judgment that Egypt experienced.

Notice what Pharaoh's response was to this awful judgment: "Pharaoh sent, and called for Moses and Aaron, and said unto them, I have sinned this time: the Lord is righteous, and I and my people are wicked. Intreat the Lord (for it is enough) that there be no more mighty thunderings and hail; and I will let you go, and ye shall stay no longer" (vv. 27,28). Although Pharaoh seemed to be conscious of his wickedness before God, it was only a feigned confession made in order to escape judgment.

Moses told Pharaoh, "As soon as I am gone out of the city, I will spread abroad my hands unto the Lord; and the thunder shall cease, neither shall there be any more hail; that thou mayest know how that the earth is the Lord's. But as for thee and thy servants, I know that ye will not yet fear the Lord God" (vv. 29,30).

Moses was not fooled by Pharaoh's false confession. God had given Moses insight so he knew what was in Pharaoh's heart and was not fooled in any way. This reveals how hardened Pharaoh really was; it did not bother him even to fake a confession of sin to God. But God knows what is in each person's heart, and He was not deceived for one minute. Chapter 9 concludes with these words: "And the heart of Pharaoh was hardened, neither would he let the children of Israel go; as the Lord had spoken by Moses" (v. 35).

God had showered His mercies on Pharaoh, but Pharaoh had refused to respond positively in any way. So in the remaining plagues God further hardened Pharaoh's heart so as to fulfill His plan of total revelation of Himself as absolutely sovereign.

The Eighth Plague

God next told Moses, "Go in unto Pharaoh: for I have hardened his heart, and the heart of his servants, that I might shew these my signs before him" (Ex. 10:1). This statement about the Lord's hardening Pharaoh's heart is also repeated in verse 20: "But the Lord hardened Pharaoh's heart, so that he would not let the children of Israel go." But as we have seen, it was only because Pharaoh had hardened his own heart that God further hardened it.

The eighth plague was one of locusts. The Bible says, "And Moses and Aaron went to Pharaoh and said to him, 'Thus says the Lord, the God of the Hebrews, "How long will you refuse to humble yourself before Me? Let My people go, that they may serve Me. For if you refuse to let My people go, behold, tomorrow I will bring locusts into your territory. And they shall cover the surface of the land, so that no one shall be able to see the land. They shall also eat the rest of what has escaped—what is left to you from the hail—and they shall eat every tree which sprouts for you out of the field.

"Then your houses shall be filled, and the houses of all your servants and the houses of all the Egyptians, something which neither your fathers nor your grandfathers have seen, from the day that they came upon the earth until this day." ' And he turned and went out from Pharaoh" (vv. 3-6, NASB).

Up to this time Moses had been content to repeat God's demand for Israel's release. However, Pharaoh's failure to keep his royal word had caused Moses to lose all respect for him in his position as king. Pharaoh's promises had been false, and his confessions of sin had produced no change in his life or attitude. Pharaoh was no longer ignorant of Jehovah, but he was willfully obstinate and defiant toward Him.

All of this caused Moses to completely alter his tone—no longer did Moses treat Pharaoh as a sovereign king but as the sinner he really was. After Moses had delivered God's pronouncement of judgment, he turned and left Pharaoh's presence, apparently without even giving him an opportunity to respond. Moses saw no further need of reasoning with Pharaoh about these matters, because Pharaoh had set his heart against God.

After Moses had left, "Pharaoh's servants said to him, 'How long will this man be a snare to us? Let the men go, that they may serve the Lord their God. Do you not realize that Egypt is destroyed?' " (v. 7, NASB). This indicates that Pharaoh's servants were more than willing to let Israel go because their country was being ruined by the plagues. But Pharaoh's heart was obstinate, and he refused to let Israel go. The battle between the king of Egypt and the God of Israel was in full force. Pharaoh was soon to find that he was no match for his opponent in this battle.

After Pharaoh's servants urged him to let the Israelites go, Pharaoh called Moses and Aaron back into his presence and offered a third proposal to them. Pharaoh said, "Go, serve the Lord your God: but who are they that shall go?" (v. 8). When Moses responded that all Israelites—young and old—with their possessions were to go (v. 9), Pharaoh charged him with having an evil plot and said, "Not so: go now ye that are men, and serve the Lord; for that ye did desire. And they were driven out from Pharaoh's presence" (v. 11). Probably no one in the Egyptian court had heard anyone stand up before the king as Moses and Aaron did.

Although Pharaoh drove Moses and Aaron from his presence, he was not rid of them or their God by any means, for next we read that the Lord told Moses, "Stretch out thine hand over the land of Egypt for the locusts, that they may come up upon the land of Egypt, and eat every herb of the land, even all that the hail hath left" (v. 12).

Moses did as the Lord instructed, "and the locusts went up over all the land of Egypt, and rested in all the coasts of

Egypt: very grievous were they; before them there were no such locusts as they, neither after them shall be such. For they covered the face of the whole earth, so that the land was darkened; and they did eat every herb of the land, and all the fruit of the trees which the hail had left: and there remained not any green thing in the trees, or in the herbs of the field, through all the land of Egypt" (vv. 14,15).

Locusts were one of the greatest terrors of the Middle East. They consumed all vegetation wherever they went. These locusts came at the bidding of God, and they would depart only at the bidding of God. They were an evident sign to Pharaoh and to the Egyptians that God was truly God. These creatures were fulfilling the secret counsels of their Creator.

During the coming time of judgment known as the Tribulation, there will also be a plague of locusts. Those who have not trusted Christ as Saviour and, therefore, are left on earth after the Rapture of the Church, will experience this judgment during the Tribulation.

This coming judgment is recorded in Revelation 9:1-6: "And the fifth angel sounded, and I saw a star from heaven which had fallen to the earth; and the key of the bottomless pit was given to him. And he opened the bottomless pit; and smoke went up out of the pit, like the smoke of a great furnace; and the sun and the air were darkened by the smoke of the pit. And out of the smoke came forth locusts upon the earth; and power was given them, as the scorpions of the earth have power.

"And they were told that they should not hurt the grass of the earth, nor any green thing, nor any tree, but only the men who do not have the seal of God on their foreheads. And they were not permitted to kill anyone, but to torment for five months; and their torment was like the torment of a scorpion when it stings a man. And in those days men will seek death and will not find it; and they will long to die and death flees from them" (NASB). We must learn that we cannot scoff at God's grace and forever escape His judgment.

After the plague of locusts on Egypt, there was nothing else Pharaoh could expect but death. That was about all that was left—everything else had been destroyed. Because of the devastation of the locusts, "Pharaoh hurriedly called for

Moses and Aaron, and he said, 'I have sinned against the Lord your God and against you. Now therefore, please forgive my sin only this once, and make supplication to the Lord your God, that He would only remove this death from me' " (Ex. 10:16,17, NASB).

Pharaoh admitted that he had sinned against both God and Moses and Aaron, and he begged them to entreat God for him just once more. How gracious and longsuffering did Pharaoh expect Moses and God to be?

But the longsuffering of God and Moses is seen in that Moses "went out from Pharaoh, and intreated the Lord. And the Lord turned a mighty strong west wind, which took away the locusts, and cast them into the Red sea; there remained not one locust in all the coasts of Egypt" (vv. 18,19). However, the following verse solemnly states, "But the Lord hardened Pharaoh's heart, so that he would not let the children of Israel go" (v. 20).

By this time, Pharaoh had sinned away his opportunity to experience God's grace. He had so hardened himself that he was no longer sensitive to God's voice. He could not expect any more mercy from God and, therefore, he was used by God to make Egypt and Israel—and all the world—see the power and majesty of God. All would gain a greater knowledge of God because of Pharaoh's hardening his heart against God.

The Ninth Plague

The ninth plague affected the sun, which was also worshiped by the Egyptians. God told Moses, "Stretch out your hand toward the heavens, that there may be darkness over the land of Egypt, a darkness which may be felt" (Ex. 10:21, Amplified).

This plague affecting the sun also revealed the power of the God of Israel over the gods of Egypt. The sun was sacred to the Egyptians, and even the name "Pharaoh" was related to a word meaning "sun."

Moses did as the Lord instructed. "And there was a thick darkness in all the land of Egypt three days" (v. 22). When the light and heat of the sun was obscured from Egypt, it meant that Egypt's most powerful god had suddenly become powerless. If the Egyptians had only realized that there was One mightier than the sun—the Creator of the sun—and that He was dealing with them in judgment!

Different explanations have been given concerning how the sun was darkened to such an extent. A sandstorm has been suggested, since the East has experienced sandstorms of such intensity that one could not see his hand in front of his face. Whatever the means, there was a darkness over Egypt of such intensity that "they saw not one another, neither rose any from his place for three days: but all the children of Israel had light in their dwellings" (v. 23).

All activity in Egypt was paralyzed, except in Goshen where God's people were unaffected. What a judgment this was on the Egyptians! Their greatest deity had deserted them, for he was powerless before the true God. No doubt many of the Egyptians wondered if they would ever see light again. What a fitting climax this plague was for the other plagues. God is light (I John 1:5), and darkness is the absence of light. Thus, this plague gave sobering evidence that Egypt was being abandoned by God and that nothing but death could possibly be expected.

The three days of darkness that Egypt experienced is a reminder of the three hours of darkness that the world experienced when Jesus Christ died on the cross to pay the penalty for sin (Matt. 27:45). When He died on the cross, the Lord Jesus Christ had all of our sin on Him. "For he hath made him to be sin for us, who knew no sin; that we might be made the righteousness of God in him" (II Cor. 5:21).

The most reasonable explanation for why the world became darkened at the time of the crucifixion was that God could not look on His Son because He had our sins on Him. Habakkuk 1:13 says of God, "Thou art of purer eyes than to behold evil, and canst not look on iniquity." While the Lord Jesus Christ had our sins on Him, the Heavenly Father covered the world with darkness so as not to look on Him. This explains why Jesus called out to the Father, "My God, my God, why hast thou forsaken me?" (Matt. 27:46). The Lord Jesus Christ was willing to go through all of this so we might have forgiveness of sin and eternal life by believing on Him as our personal Saviour.

While the Egyptians were experiencing a darkness so great that it could be felt, the Israelites were experiencing the brightness of God's blessing. The Bible does not explain how there could be darkness on the Egyptians and light on the Israelites at the same time, but the all-powerful God would not have difficulty in accomplishing this task. While the Egyptians were living in a darkness which could not be lighted, the Israelites had a light which could not be darkened.

Although this was true physically of the Egyptians and the Israelites, it is also true spiritually of those who reject God and those who believe God. Since God is light, those who trust Jesus Christ as personal Saviour are children of light. But those who do not trust Jesus Christ as Saviour are children of darkness.

John 3:18,19 says, "He that believeth on him is not condemned: but he that believeth not is condemned already, because he hath not believed in the name of the only begotten Son of God. And this is the condemnation, that light is come into the world, and men loved darkness rather than light, because their deeds were evil."

There is light in the presence of the Lord, but separation from Him brings darkness. The Bible explains what the Lord Jesus Christ will do when He returns to earth to establish His kingdom: "In flaming fire taking vengeance on them that know not God, and that obey not the gospel of our Lord Jesus Christ: who shall be punished with everlasting destruction from the presence of the Lord, and from the glory of his power" (II Thess. 1:8,9). No wonder Hebrews 10:31 says, "It is a fearful thing to fall into the hands of the living God."

But the good news is that Jesus Christ has paid for our sin, and if we trust Him as Saviour we will be delivered from condemnation and darkness. Colossians 1:13 says that God "hath delivered us from the power of darkness, and hath translated us into the kingdom of his dear Son." So as we consider the matter of light and darkness, let us not forget how the subject relates to the Person of God. "This then is the message which we have heard of him, and declare unto you, that God is light, and in him is no darkness at all" (I John 1:5).

When the judgment of darkness came on Egypt, Pharaoh called for Moses and told him, "Go, serve the Lord; only let your flocks and your herds be detained. Even your little ones may go with you" (Ex. 10:24, NASB). This was Pharaoh's fourth and final compromise offer. Pharaoh wasn't dumb; he realized that people are attached to their property and that if the Egyptians could keep the property of the Israelites, then they could be assured that the Israelites would return. But Moses was not about to accept a compromise offer. He said, "Not a hoof will be left behind" (v. 26, NASB).

Pharaoh was now past feeling, and the omniscient God also knew that he was unchangeable. Thus, the Bible says again, "But the Lord made Pharaoh's heart stronger and more stubborn, and he would not let them go" (v. 27, Amplified).

Then the proud king, unchanged by all of these judgments, said to Moses, "Get away from me! See that you never enter my presence again, for the day you see my face again you shall die!" (v. 28, Amplified). Moses answered Pharaoh, "Thou hast spoken well, I will see thy face again no more" (v. 29).

Although Moses was normally a tranquil person, at that point he expressed himself strongly and emphatically to Pharaoh. Moses then delivered the announcement of the tenth plague that was to come on Pharaoh. Then "he went out from Pharaoh in a great anger" (11:8). Because Moses had his eyes fixed on God, he did not fear the wrath of the king (see Heb. 11:27).

The announcement that Moses gave Pharaoh concerning the final plague was a revelation that God had given Moses when He called him at the burning bush. God knew this plague would be necessary, and the time had finally come. The Lord told Moses, "Yet will I bring one plague more upon Pharaoh, and upon Egypt; afterwards he will let you go hence; when he shall let you go, he shall surely thrust you out hence altogether" (Ex. 11:1).

I can just see Moses as he raised himself to his full height and poured an overwhelming torrent of denunciation and warning on Pharaoh and announced his and Egypt's doom. Moses said, " 'Thus says the Lord, "About midnight I am going out into the midst of Egypt, and all the first-born in the land of Egypt shall die, from the first-born of the

Pharaoh who sits on his throne, even to the first-born of the slave girl who is behind the millstones; all the first-born of the cattle as well.

"Moreover, there shall be a great cry in all the land of Egypt, such as there has not been before and such as shall never be again. But against any of the sons of Israel a dog shall not even bark, whether against man or beast, that you may understand how the Lord makes a distinction between Egypt and Israel." And all of these your servants will come down to me and bow themselves before me, saying, "Go out, you and all the people who follow you," and after that I will go out.' And he went out from Pharaoh in hot anger" (vv. 4-8, NASB).

We have previously considered the significance of the statement that not even a dog would bark at the Israelites as they prepared to leave Egypt. This was a miracle in itself. It showed again the great distinction that God made between His people and the Egyptians.

The last time that Moses saw Pharaoh's face was when he announced this judgment. Moses had been faithful to the work God had called him to do; he had delivered instructions to Pharaoh precisely as God gave them. Thus, Exodus 11:3 says, "Moreover the man Moses was very great in the land of Egypt, in the sight of Pharaoh's servants, and in the sight of the people."

But in spite of the announcement that the firstborn of those who did not believe God and act on the basis of their belief would be killed, the Lord told Moses, "Pharaoh shall not hearken unto you; that my wonders may be multiplied in the land of Egypt" (v. 9). After the tenth plague came on Pharaoh and the Egyptians, they begged the Israelites to leave their country.

These nine plagues had accomplished the purposes of God. The Egyptian gods were proven to be fraudulent, the Lord God was proven true and all powerful, Pharaoh was proven to be one of the "vessels of wrath fitted to destruction" (Rom. 9:22), and Moses was proven to be a great and powerful servant of God.

Chapter 7

The Progressive Compromises of Pharaoh

Having considered the increasing intensity of the plagues, we want to now examine the compromises offered by Pharaoh as these plagues were brought on him and the Egyptians.

As frequently pointed out, when Moses and Aaron first came to Pharaoh, he would not obey the Lord or even give Him recognition. Pharaoh said, "Who is the Lord, that I should obey his voice to let Israel go? I know not the Lord, neither will I let Israel go" (Ex. 5:2). Pharaoh also referred to the words of God spoken through Moses and Aaron as vain, or idle, words (see v. 9).

Even though Moses received this strong reaction from Pharaoh, he knew what God had already said concerning the judgments He would bring on Pharaoh and the Egyptians. It must have been apparent to Moses even at this time that he would have to exercise patience in waiting on Pharaoh, yet he knew there was no need to compromise God's requirements since God would perform His will in spite of Pharaoh.

We must learn this important lesson also. We do not have to compromise with Satan, for we have the promise of God that He will give us victory in the end as we allow Him to work in our lives. As we are faced with adverse circumstances, we can know that God is accomplishing in our lives what is for our best and for His glory.

Romans 8:28,29 reminds us of this: "And we know that all things work together for good to them that love God, to them who are the called according to his purpose. For whom he did foreknow, he also did predestinate to be conformed to the image of his Son." Thus, God allows difficult things to come into our lives so that He can make us more like Jesus Christ.

For the Christian, there is victory. This is why the Apostle Paul said in the same chapter of Romans, "What shall we then say to these things? If God be for us, who can be against us? He that spared not his own Son, but delivered him up for us all, how shall he not with him also freely give us all things? Who shall lay anything to the charge of God's elect? It is God that justifieth. Who is he that condemneth? It is Christ that died, yea rather, that is risen again, who is even at the right hand of God, who also maketh intercession for us" (vv. 31-34).

The believer has no reason whatever to give in to any of Satan's compromises. The Lord Jesus Christ provides everything we need to live a godly life and to resist the advances of Satan.

We can count on the Lord Jesus Christ to do His work in our lives. Philippians 1:6 says, "Being confident of this very thing, that he which hath begun a good work in you will perform it until the day of Jesus Christ." When is the "day of Jesus Christ"? It will be the day when He returns to take His own to heaven to be with Himself. But until then, He will continue to perform the work He has begun in us.

The Bible emphasizes that Jesus Christ is all that we need. This truth is especially seen in I Corinthians 1:30: "But of him are ye in Christ Jesus, who of God is made unto us wisdom, and righteousness, and sanctification, and redemption." Since Christ is all we need, we can say with the Apostle Paul, "Thanks be to God, which giveth us the victory through our Lord Jesus Christ. Therefore, my beloved brethren, be ye stedfast, unmoveable, always abounding in the work of the Lord, forasmuch as ye know that your labour is not in vain in the Lord" (15:57,58).

There is always triumph in Jesus Christ. Why? Because of what He accomplished when He died on the cross for us. Hebrews 2:14,15 reveals that Christ broke the power of Satan over us, enabling us to experience victory in Christ. That is why James 4:7 says, "Submit yourselves therefore to God. Resist the devil, and he will flee from you." We should take this firm stand; we do not need to accept any compromises that Satan offers us.

Because Pharaoh would not obey God or even recognize Him, he and the land of Egypt began to experience plagues. The purpose of these plagues was to cause Pharaoh to see the need of recognizing and obeying God. But not until after the progressive severity of the first four plagues was Pharaoh even willing to discuss the possibility of the Israelites' leaving Egypt.

First Compromise Offer

After the fourth judgment, which was the plague of swarms of insects on the entire land of Egypt, Pharaoh called for Moses and Aaron and told them, "Go ye, sacrifice to your God in the land" (Ex. 8:25). The key word to notice is "in." Pharaoh did not want them to leave the land but to sacrifice within the boundaries of Egypt. He saw no reason why the Israelites could not make sacrifices to their God in the land where they were living.

Pharaoh's offer to Moses also contains a lesson for us. The counterpart to the suggestion he was making is heard today and is expressed something like this: "You can be as religious as you want, but don't become so narrow that you make a complete break with the world." In other words, be a Christian if you have to be, but keep on living like the world lives. To follow such a philosophy is to be conformed to the world and to its way of thinking.

Pharaoh did not insist that Israel bow down to his gods, so in a sense he did make them a "reasonable" offer. Surely, he reasoned, they can carry on their religion here as well as anyplace else; there's room for everyone, so why demand a complete separation?

If Moses had accepted Pharaoh's compromise offer, Israel would have been placed on the same level with Egypt and the God of Israel on the same level as the gods of Egypt. The Egyptians could then have said, "We see no difference between us—you have your worship, and we have our worship—it's all alike." And this is what many are thinking today; they fail to see the distinction between Christianity and religion because so many believers have not really separated themselves from the world.

As a result, some say, "It doesn't matter what you believe, just as long as you are sincere. We are all going to the same place, so why be so separated?" But what does the Bible say? John 14:6 records the words of Christ: "I am the way, the truth, and the life: no man cometh unto the Father, but by me." Acts 4:12 says, "Neither is there salvation in any other: for there is none other name under heaven given among men, whereby we must be saved." So there is a sharp distinction between Christianity and religion; Christianity is a right relationship with a person—the Lord Jesus Christ.

Throughout the Scriptures, Egypt represents the world. The Israelites were frequently warned not to go down to Egypt because this was, in effect, relying on the arm of flesh rather than relying on God. The "world" refers to people or a way of thinking that ignores God. Galatians 1:4 says that Christ "gave himself for our sins, that he might deliver us from this present evil world."

Although Christians are *in* the world, they are not *of* the world. Jesus told His followers, "If ye were of the world, the world would love his own: but because ye are not of the world, but I have chosen you out of the world, therefore the world hateth you" (John 15:19). Notice the strong words of James 4:4: "Ye adulterers and adulteresses, know ye not that the friendship of the world is enmity with God? Whosoever therefore will be a friend of the world is the enemy of God."

Although we do not wish to be disliked by anyone, we must obey the injunction to "go forth therefore unto him without the camp, bearing his reproach" (Heb. 13:13). If we are going to please God in our daily walk, it is necessary for us to be separate from the world. This is why the Bible says, "Wherefore come out from among them, and be ye separate, saith the Lord, and touch not the unclean thing; and I will receive you, and will be a Father unto you, and ye shall be my sons and daughters, saith the Lord Almighty" (II Cor. 6:17,18).

When Pharaoh made his first compromise offer, Moses firmly replied, "It is not right to do so, for we shall sacrifice to the Lord our God what is an abomination to the Egyptians. If we sacrifice what is an abomination to the Egyptians before their eyes, will they not then stone us? We must go a three days' journey into the wilderness and sacrifice to the Lord our God as He commands us" (Ex. 8:26,27, NASB). Inasmuch as the Egyptians considered certain animals to be sacred, they would have been highly offended if the Israelites had killed those animals as an offering; it would have been considered a sacrilege. The worship of the Israelites was utter foolishness to them.

This reminds us of what Paul said in I Corinthians 1:18: "For the preaching of the cross is to them that perish foolishness; but unto us which are saved it is the power of God." Paul also said, "We preach Christ crucified, unto the Jews a stumblingblock, and unto the Greek foolishness; but unto them which are called, both Jews and Greeks, Christ the power of God, and the wisdom of God. Because the foolishness of God is wiser than men; and the weakness of God is stronger than men" (vv. 23-25).

First Corinthians 2:14 says, "But a natural man does not accept the things of the Spirit of God; for they are foolishness to him, and he cannot understand them, because they are spiritually appraised" (NASB). Spiritual truths can be discerned only by those who are in right relationship to Jesus Christ; an unbeliever is not able to evaluate spiritual truths.

A believer recognizes that all he has is due to what Christ has accomplished for him on the cross. This is what caused Paul to say, "But God forbid that I should glory, save in the cross of our Lord Jesus Christ, by whom the world is crucified unto me, and I unto the world" (Gal. 6:14). This verse reveals that if we have accepted Christ as Saviour, we have died to the world and are to take our place as dead to the world.

We cannot expect anything good to come from the world. This is why the Lord Jesus said, "If the world hate you, ye know that it hated me before it hated you. If ye were of the world, the world would love his own: but because ye are not of the world, but I have chosen you out of the world, therefore the world hateth you. Remember the word that I said unto you, The servant is not greater than his lord. If they have persecuted me, they will also persecute you; if they have kept my saying, they will keep your's also" (John 15:18-20).

Moses' refusal to accept Pharaoh's compromise offer revealed that Moses clearly understood the necessity of a

complete separation between Israel and Egypt if Israel was to
serve God as He desired. Far too many people try to serve
God and cling to the things of the world at the same time.
Far too few are able to identify with I John 3:1: "Behold,
what manner of love the Father hath bestowed upon us, that
we should be called the sons of God: therefore the world
knoweth us not, because it knew him not." What a shame it
is that so many believers want recognition from the world as
well as recognition from God.

As he responded to Pharaoh, Moses clearly understood
that he was under orders from God. Moses said they would
sacrifice to God "as he shall command us" (Ex. 8:27). How
wonderful it is when a believer has a clear comprehension of
God's will for his life. This is something that Satan likes to
confuse and neutralize—as he successfully did in the Garden
of Eden.

When we know that God has spoken, that should settle
the matter for us. But it did not settle it for Eve; she was
completely deceived by Satan. And often the fact that God
has spoken does not settle anything for a believer who is
deceived by the temptations of the world. But God has
clearly instructed that we are not to be a friend of the world.
The world and the believer have nothing in common, and the
believer who is a friend of the world is committing spiritual
adultery.

The Book of Colossians tells believers that we are not
only dead to the world, but we are alive to Christ. "If ye then
be risen with Christ, seek those things which are above, where
Christ sitteth on the right hand of God" (3:1). In other
words, we are to apply, or fix, our minds on heavenly things.
The passage goes on to say, "Set your affection on things
above, not on things on the earth. For ye are dead, and your
life is hid with Christ in God" (vv. 2,3). When a person trusts
Jesus Christ as Saviour, he dies to the world and is made alive
to Jesus Christ.

Second Compromise Offer

After his first compromise offer was declined, Pharaoh
said to Moses, "I will let you go, that you may sacrifice to
the Lord your God in the wilderness; only you shall not go

very far away. Make supplication for me" (Ex. 8:28, NASB).
This was really only a modification of the first compromise
offer, and it was even more subtle than Pharaoh's first
suggestion. The Enemy does not like the believer to be out of
his sight. Keeping the Israelites close would have allowed
Pharaoh and the Egyptians to control them. Pharaoh was not
really yielding to God's demand that he let the Israelites go.

It is understandable that Pharaoh was not easily
persuaded to let the Israelites go; they were his slaves, and he
gained much by having them in his country. He was willing to
lengthen their "chains" so they could go a little distance into
the wilderness, but he did not want to lose control of them
completely.

This reminds us of one of the greatest temptations a
Christian faces—some are always urging him not to be
fanatical in what he believes. It's all right with them if he
wants to be religious, but they encourage him not to take his
Christianity too seriously. The implication is that you should
not let Christianity spoil your life. Some say, "I don't mix
my religion with my business." This is a trick of the Devil
that causes a person to attempt to hang on to the world while
still endeavoring to live for Christ. The one who has
genuinely trusted Christ as Saviour should recognize that he
owes everything to Christ and nothing to the world.

Some think the believer will lose all joy if he becomes too
serious about his Christianity. But those who are long faced
and miserable are not the ones who have separated
completely from the world; rather, they are those who have
compromised with the world and have a troubled conscience.
An individual's church attendance sometimes indicates that
he is far more concerned about enjoying the pleasures of this
world on weekends than he is about fellowshiping with other
believers and hearing the teaching of the Word of God. So
maintaining a border position suits the purpose of the Enemy
very well. Satan is thus able to keep the person from being
totally committed to either position.

Moses had been sent to Pharaoh for the single purpose of
leading the children of Israel out of Egypt, and he was not
about to compromise, no matter how small that compromise
may have been. May we also learn the importance of carrying
out God's clear commands without compromising with the

Enemy. When we know that we have done what the Lord wants us to do, we will experience a joy that is beyond comparison.

The Lord Jesus Christ came into this world so that He might lead us out of it. This does not mean that He is going to take us to heaven right away. Those of us who trust Him as Saviour are given a task to do, and that is why He leaves us on earth. If we had no task, it would be better for us to die the moment we trust Him as Saviour so we would be taken to heaven to be with Him.

The Lord Jesus leaves us here not only so that we can proclaim the message of salvation to others but also so that He can mature us in the Christian faith. And part of the maturing process is to realize that, as believers, we are to be separated from the world. We are not to be yoked together with unbelievers.

The Bible says, "Do not be bound together with unbelievers; for what partnership have righteousness and lawlessness, or what fellowship has light with darkness? Or what harmony has Christ with Belial, or what has a believer in common with an unbeliever? Or what agreement has the temple of God with idols? For we are the temple of the living God; just as God said, 'I will dwell in them and walk among them; and I will be their God, and they shall be My people. Therefore, come out from their midst and be separate, says the Lord' " (II Cor. 6:14-17, NASB). Although believers are in the world, they are not to be of the world.

Because Moses understood the principle of separation from the world, he did not even respond when Pharaoh made the compromise suggestion that the Israelites go into the wilderness but that they not "go very far away" (Ex. 8:28). In Moses' mind no compromise was possible because God had said He was going to lead them out and take them to Himself. This reveals that the promises of God give us strength to stand against compromising suggestions. We will not compromise our standards as long as we keep God's commands before us.

In the Scriptures separation involves two aspects. There is separation *from* whatever is contrary to the will of God, and there is separation *to* God Himself. Being separated from the world does not mean that we lose contact with it. Worldliness is not simply contact with the world; it is complying with or comforming to the world. When we are separated from the world and separated to God, the reward is incomparable communion and fellowship with God.

In His great prayer for His own, the Lord Jesus Christ said, "I do not ask Thee to take them out of the world, but to keep them from the evil one" (John 17:15, NASB).

Third Compromise Offer

Pharaoh's third compromise offer was made after the seventh plague, which was a plague of thunder, hail and fire. The offer was made after Moses had announced the coming plague of locusts. Pharaoh and the Egyptians had never experienced anything like what Moses predicted. Egypt was in ruins because of the previous plagues, and Pharaoh and the Egyptians could imagine what a plague of locusts would do to their country. Moses said that the locusts "shall fill thy houses, and the houses of all thy servants, and the houses of all the Egyptians; which neither thy fathers, nor thy fathers' fathers have seen, since the day that they were upon the earth unto this day" (Ex. 10:6).

Such a pronouncement of judgment caused Pharaoh's servants to say to him, "How long shall this man be a snare unto us? Let the men go, that they may serve the Lord their God: knowest thou not yet that Egypt is destroyed?" (v. 7). Pharaoh then called Moses and Aaron and said to them, "Go, serve the Lord your God; but who are to go?" (v. 8, Berkeley). Moses replied that young and old, sons and daughters, flocks and herds were going so that all could participate in a feast to the Lord (v. 9).

Pharaoh then presented his third compromise offer: "May the Lord be with you if I intend to let you and your little ones go! Look out! You are plotting mischief! No, indeed! You men go and serve the Lord, for that is what you wanted!" (vv. 10,11, Berkeley). Having said this to Moses and Aaron, Pharaoh then drove them out of his presence.

This amounted to a test concerning natural affection. Pharaoh approved of the men going but implied that they should not interfere with the worldly advancements of their families. This compromise demands our special attention because the test involved is common today.

Many think it is unreasonable for parents to expect their children to conform to their standards. The implication is that parents have outmoded standards and that it is unreasonable to expect the younger generation to live by them. But families cannot live by two different standards. This is as unreasonable as the Egyptians expecting the Israelite men to worship in the wilderness while their families remained in Egypt. Children are actually loaned to parents by God, and we parents are responsible for training them to live as they should. This is an awesome responsibility, for what we sow in their lives we will later reap. Galatians 6:7,8 states a timeless principle: "Do not be deceived, God is not mocked; for whatever a man sows, this he will also reap. For the one who sows to his own flesh shall from the flesh reap corruption, but the one who sows to the Spirit shall from the Spirit reap eternal life" (NASB).

Ephesians 6:4 admonishes, "Fathers, do not provoke your children to anger; but bring them up in the discipline and instruction of the Lord" (NASB). Perhaps the most familiar biblical text on child training is Proverbs 22:6: "Train up a child in the way he should go: and when he is old, he will not depart from it." These are God's words, not man's ideas.

Pharaoh was wise enough to know that if the Israelite men left their families in Egypt, they would return to the families, because their love would draw them back. Pharaoh took into account the strong bonds within the family. Regrettably, those bonds are growing weaker today. It seems that many parents could not care less about what happens to their children, particularly regarding spiritual training. No doubt this is because many Christian parents are still spiritually "in Egypt" and are occupied with the things of this world rather than with eternal matters. All believers ought to live with eternity's values in view.

It is wonderful that parents are concerned about providing materially for their children, but some parents see only the material needs of their children. However, things never truly satisfy. And often, in the end, the children resent their parents, who gave them things but did not give of themselves. Christian parents should not only be concerned about giving their time and attention to their children, but they should also help their children develop a proper relationship with the Lord.

The rearing of our children is our direct responsibility, and we must never think that we can shift that responsibility to someone else. Because of certain circumstances in our lives, we may have to rely on others for help, but we must always recognize that the responsibility is directly ours.

Unfortunately, family discipline has been relaxed today to the extent that there is hardly any discipline at all. The Scriptures are not given their proper place in the home. Children are allowed to choose their own companions, and many Christian parents seem to make no serious effort to bring their children out of spiritual Egypt. Perhaps the reason for this is that many of the parents themselves are still in spiritual Egypt.

The training of children is a solemn responsibility, and in these days of laxity and lawlessness, proper training of children is an ever-increasing problem. When Pharaoh suggested that the Israelites leave their families in Egypt, Moses probably thought of his own childhood training and remembered how thoroughly his own parents had done their job.

As we think of parental responsibility, we learn from Joshua about the leadership that a Christian parent should exercise in his family. Joshua said to the Israelites, "If it is disagreeable in your sight to serve the Lord, choose for yourselves today whom you will serve: whether the gods which your fathers served which were beyond the River, or the Gods of the Amorites in whose land you are living; but as for me and my house, we will serve the Lord" (Josh. 24:15, NASB).

In our own home Mrs. Epp and I trained our children in spiritual truths from the time they were able to understand. They were taught Bible verses and Bible stories, as well as hymns and gospel songs. We had a regular devotional time, and the children simply grew up in this atmosphere. Later, when they became teenagers and considered further schooling, it was a common understanding that they would go to Bible school first. They all did this, and some later went on to further schooling. I say this only to point out that it is necessary to begin a child's spiritual training at the earliest age.

The Apostle Paul reminded Timothy, "From a child thou hast known the holy scriptures, which are able to make thee wise unto salvation through faith which is in Christ Jesus" (II Tim. 3:15). Some parents do not come to know Christ as Saviour until their children are older, but those parents who know Christ when their children are young should start spiritual training early. Although we have many wonderful Sunday schools and even Christian child care centers, the parents are directly responsible for the training of their children.

The suggestion that the Israelites leave their families in Egypt can be compared to present-day parents leaving their children in spiritual Egypt. It would be the same as permitting their children to have their own way, allowing them to conform to the world, permitting them to grow up without the fear of the Lord, neglecting their spiritual training and simply ignoring God's command that parents bring their children up "in the nurture and admonition of the Lord" (Eph. 6:4).

We are not going to warp the personalities of our children if we restrain them, nor are we going to warp their characters by diligently teaching them truths concerning God at a very early age. Within the heart of every individual is the desire to learn about God. This fact is indicated in Ecclesiastes 3:11: "He has made everything appropriate in its time. He has also set eternity in their heart" (NASB). Within the heart of each individual is a vacuum that only the knowledge of and proper relationship to God can fill. It is important, therefore, that parents not neglect the spiritual training of their children.

How refreshing it is to see a parent who is faithful in his family responsibility. Each Christian parent should desire to have said of him what God said of Abraham: "For I know him, that he will command his children and his household after him, and they shall keep the way of the Lord" (Gen. 18:19). Before the Israelites entered the land of Canaan, God gave them these clear instructions: "These words, which I command thee this day, shall be in thine heart: and thou shalt teach them diligently unto thy children, and shalt talk

of them when thou sittest in thine house, and when thou
walkest by the way, and when thou liest down, and when
thou risest up" (Deut. 6:6,7).

So in response to Pharaoh's question concerning who
planned to leave Egypt, Moses said everyone was to go,
young and old alike. Moses had a firm answer because he
knew God's will and wanted to be faithful to it.

Fourth Compromise Offer

Pharaoh's fourth offer was made to Moses during the
ninth plague, which was a plague of terrible darkness.
Pharaoh called for Moses and said, "You go and serve the
Lord; only leave your flocks and herds behind, while you
take your little ones along" (Ex. 10:24, Berkeley).

This last compromise offer by Pharaoh was an appeal to
coveteousness. It was an attempt to get Moses to separate his
relationship with the Lord from his business activity. Satan
plants the same idea in the minds of believers today. It is not
uncommon to hear of those who boast that they do not let
their religious activities mix with their business activities.
This reveals the perseverance with which Satan disputes our
separation to God.

Since Pharaoh could not convince Moses and the
Israelites to sacrifice in the land of Egypt, he tried to
convince them to leave the land of Egypt without taking
anything along to offer as sacrifices to God. Had they left
Egypt without their livestock, they would have been unable
to really worship the Lord as He intended.

In this compromise offer we see Satan's attempt to divide
the loyalties of the heart so a person will try to serve two
masters. The Bible contains many examples of those who had
divided loyalties. The Apostle Paul wrote concerning a
former companion, "Demas hath forsaken me, having loved
this present world" (II Tim. 4:10).

But in contrast to such a person, note what Paul said
concerning Timothy: "I hope in the Lord Jesus to send
Timothy to you shortly, so that I also may be encouraged
when I learn of your condition. For I have no one else of
kindred spirit who will genuinely be concerned for your
welfare. For they all seek after their own interests, not those

of Christ Jesus. But you know of his proven worth that he served with me in the furtherance of the gospel like a child serving his father" (Phil. 2:19-22, NASB).

Ananias and Sapphira had divided loyalties to the extent that they even lied to God. Acts 5 tells how they sold property and claimed to give the full price when they had actually held back part of it. The sin was not keeping part of the price of the land, for they were not required to give the full price. Rather, the sin was lying about giving the full price. This was the sin of pretense. But such sins happen when a person's treasures are in spiritual Egypt, which also causes his affections to remain there.

The important question really is, Does God have the title to all that you possess? Some feel that only a tenth belongs to the Lord, and the rest belongs to them. The right perspective, however, is to realize that everything we have comes from the Lord; therefore, everything belongs to Him.

Of course, as far as the government is concerned, we own everything we possess. But the Christian realizes that everything he has comes from the hand of God. God has said, "For every beast of the forest is mine, and the cattle upon a thousand hills. I know all the fowls of the mountains: and the wild beasts of the field are mine. If I were hungry, I would not tell thee: for the world is mine, and the fulness thereof" (Ps. 50:10-12).

Deuteronomy 10:14 says, "Behold, the heaven and the heaven of heavens is the Lord's thy God, the earth also, with all that therein is." Along this same line, Psalm 24:1 declares, "The earth is the Lord's, and the fulness thereof; the world and they that dwell therein." The New Testament echoes this same truth: "For the earth is the Lord's, and the fulness thereof" (I Cor. 10:26).

Many Christians fail God in the area of their possessions. The emphasis of our materialistic age is, "Give yourself to God if you must, but do not consecrate your possessions to His service." This kind of thinking originates with Satan himself. How tragic it is that some Christians have been enabled by God to accumulate many possessions, and yet they do not consecrate them to the Lord.

Although we are not now living under the Mosaic Law, we need to remember the solemn charge that God gave to

Israel: "Will a man rob God? Yet you are robbing Me! But you say, 'How have we robbed Thee?' In tithes and contributions. You are cursed with a curse, for you are robbing Me, the whole nation of you!" (Mal. 3:8,9, NASB). We are not living under the Law, so the regulation of the tithe is not directly binding on us. However, the principle of giving back to God a portion of what He has given to us should still apply. If a tithe was required under the Law, surely we should be willing to do as much under grace! Are we holding back offerings that belong to God? If so, God will not bless our lives.

In answer to Pharaoh's suggestion that the Israelites leave their livestock in Egypt, Moses firmly declared, "Our livestock must therefore come with us; not a hoof shall be left behind, because from them we shall take to serve the Lord our God, and we do not know what to use for the Lord's service until we reach there" (Ex. 10:26, Berkeley). Moses took a firm stand on putting everything at God's disposal; he would not leave anything in Egypt.

Moses told Pharaoh that they did not know what they would use for the Lord's service until they reached their destination. This statement gives us insight into how Moses determined the will of God. He realized that the mind of God could not be discerned so long as they left anything in Egypt. Moses realized that he and the Israelites had to leave Egypt with all of their possessions. Then—and only then—would they know what the Lord's will for service really was.

It is a time-honored principle of God that we must be willing to obey before He will reveal His will to us. John 7:17 says, "If any man will do his will, he shall know of the doctrine, whether it be of God, or whether I speak of myself." This means that we must be willing to lay everything on the altar; we must present ourselves to God with no strings attached.

Paul said it in these words: "I urge you therefore, brethren, by the mercies of God, to present your bodies a living and holy sacrifice, acceptable to God, which is your spiritual service of worship. And do not be conformed to this world, but be transformed by the renewing of your mind, that you may prove what the will of God is, that which is good and acceptable and perfect" (Rom. 12:1,2, NASB).

Some Christians ask, "What does God want me to do?" Some say, "Lord, I would present all my goods to You if I only knew what You want me to do with them." But that's not God's method. He does not reveal His will to us until we put everything at His disposal—ourselves first of all.

Moses absolutely resisted any temptation to compromise with Pharaoh by leaving any livestock behind. With clear spiritual insight, Moses saw through every compromise offer extended by Pharaoh, and his reply was clear and decisive in each case. From all of this, we can see the necessity for absolute obedience to God. The call of God is to separation—complete separation. Just as Moses insisted, we also need to devote to God everything He has given us and to use it for His glory.

The world urges us to remain in the land and to be neighborly, but we have only one obligation—to be separated to God. We must always remember that "friendship of the world is enmity with God" (James 4:4). Romans 8:7,8 emphasizes the same truth: "Because the mind set on the flesh is hostile toward God; for it does not subject itself to the Law of God, for it is not even able to do so; and those who are in the flesh cannot please God" (NASB). One who lives by the standards of the world, or his old nature, does not please God in any way.

Although he lived long before these New Testament verses were ever penned, Moses grasped this spiritual truth and totally refused any compromise offer from Pharaoh. Moses boldly told Pharaoh that not even a hoof would be left behind (Ex. 10:26).

Such a response made Pharaoh angry. He said to Moses, "Get away from me and see to it that you never come near me again; for if I ever see you again, you die!" (v. 28, Berkeley). But even these words did not frighten Moses. " 'Correctly spoken,' Moses retorted, 'you will not see me again' " (v. 29, Berkeley).

Moses was able to face Pharaoh as he did only because he was in right relationship to God and realized that no compromise would be acceptable to God. Moses had laid everything on the altar as far as his worship of and service to God was concerned. Have you done the same? Or do you have divided loyalties between the world and God? The believer experiences deeply satisfying joy only when he is separated from the world and is separated to God.

Chapter 8

The Final Judgment

After the ninth plague, Pharaoh was so angry with Moses that he told him to leave and stay away—and threatened that if he ever saw Moses again he would kill him (Ex. 10:28). Moses agreed with Pharaoh that he would never see him again (v. 29).

Before leaving Pharaoh, however, Moses announced God's final judgment on Pharaoh and the Egyptians. Although the nature of this judgment was news to Pharaoh, it was not new to Moses because God had told him about it before any of the plagues began. When God called Moses at the burning bush in the desert, He said to him, "When thou goest to return into Egypt, see that thou do all those wonders before Pharaoh, which I have put in thine hand: but I will harden his heart, that he shall not let the people go. And thou shalt say unto Pharaoh, Thus saith the Lord, Israel is my son, even my firstborn: and I say unto thee, Let my son go, that he may serve me: and if thou refuse to let him go, behold, I will slay thy son, even thy firstborn" (4:21-23).

But in spite of the fact that God, in His omniscience, knew that He would finally have to bring this judgment on Pharaoh, He still demonstrated much longsuffering and mercy to Pharaoh. God gave Pharaoh many opportunities to repent and turn to Him, but Pharaoh absolutely refused to do so. Because Pharaoh and Egypt had not heeded God's commands or responded to His mercy, God brought this final judgment on them.

This reminds us of how graciously God deals with lost sinners concerning salvation. It is also a reminder of how graciously He deals with believers concerning yielding totally

107

to Him. God is longsuffering and full of mercy, but if He is rejected, He must finally act in judgment or discipline, depending on whether the person is an unbeliever or a believer. Although we do not know when that time is, there apparently comes a day when God says, "I will wait no longer." And remember, "It is a fearful thing to fall into the hands of the living God" (Heb. 10:31).

The Bible reveals that judgment awaits those who refuse God's mercy and reject Christ as Saviour. Hebrews 9:27 says, "It is appointed unto men once to die, but after this the judgment." Proverbs 29:1 warns, "He, that being often reproved hardeneth his neck, shall suddenly be destroyed, and that without remedy." Second Thessalonians 1:8,9 tells how the unsaved will be destroyed when Christ returns to earth: "In flaming fire taking vengeance on them that know not God, and that obey not the gospel of our Lord Jesus Christ: who shall be punished with everlasting destruction from the presence of the Lord, and from the glory of his power."

The final judgment of all the unsaved will take place before the Great White Throne. Revelation 20:11-15 says, "And I saw a great white throne and Him who sat upon it, from whose presence earth and heaven fled away, and no place was found for them. And I saw the dead, the great and the small, standing before the throne, and books were opened; and another book was opened, which is the book of life; and the dead were judged from the things which were written in the books, according to their deeds.

"And the sea gave up the dead which were in it, and death and Hades gave up the dead which were in them; and they were judged, every one of them according to their deeds. And death and Hades were thrown into the lake of fire. This is the second death, the lake of fire. And if anyone's name was not found written in the book of life, he was thrown into the lake of fire" (NASB).

So it is tremendously important for each person to respond to God's longsuffering and mercy while there is still time. Hebrews 3:7-9 pleads, "Therefore, just as the Holy Spirit says, 'Today if you hear His voice, do not harden your hearts as when they provoked Me, as in the day of trial in the wilderness, where your fathers tried Me by testing Me, and saw My works for forty years' " (NASB).

Those who lift their hearts in pride against God, as did Pharaoh, will be brought low. All must someday give recognition to Jesus Christ whether they have trusted Him as Saviour or not. This truth is emphasized in Philippians 2:9-11: "Wherefore God also hath highly exalted him, and given him a name which is above every name: that at the name of Jesus every knee should bow, of things in heaven, and things in earth, and things under the earth; and that every tongue should confess that Jesus Christ is Lord, to the glory of God the Father."

The contest between Pharaoh and Jehovah was almost ended. There had been abundant opportunity for Pharaoh to repent of his haughty defiance, but he refused to do so. There had been warning after warning and plague after plague, but Pharaoh's heart was still hardened. Therefore, after God had again confirmed this hardness, He brought the final plague on Pharaoh and the Egyptians.

Announcement of the Final Plague

Moses' announcement of the final plague is recorded in Exodus 11. Verse 1 is the key to understanding its purpose: "The Lord said unto Moses, Yet will I bring one plague more upon Pharaoh, and upon Egypt; afterwards he will let you go hence; when he shall let you go, he shall surely thrust you out hence altogether." Not only would Pharaoh be willing to let the Israelites go, he would actually push them out of his country. This reveals the folly of fighting against God, because He finally brings a person to his knees. The creature is impotent before his omnipotent Creator.

Proverbs 19:21 says, "There are many devices in a man's heart; nevertheless the counsel of the Lord, that shall stand." Because God is omnipotent, He was able to accomplish with Pharaoh what He pleased. "The king's heart is in the hand of the Lord, as the rivers of water: he turneth it whithersoever he will" (Prov. 21:1). Isaiah 14:27 emphasizes this same truth: "For the Lord of hosts hath purposed, and who shall disannul it? And his hand is stretched out, and who shall turn it back?"

Even Pharaoh—the king of the most powerful empire in the world—was not able to successfully resist God. Pharaoh eventually had to recognize what King Nebuchadnezzar later recognized: "Those that walk in pride he [God] is able to abase" (Dan. 4:37).

But Pharaoh's heart was hardened against God because he refused from the beginning to obey God or to even give recognition to Him (Ex. 5:2). What Pharaoh did not realize was that God can grind to powder the hardest heart and completely humble the haughtiest spirit.

The Lord said to Moses, "Speak now in the hearing of the people, and let every man solicit and ask of his neighbor, and every woman of her neighbor, jewels of silver and jewels of gold. And the Lord gave the people favor in the sight of the Egyptians. Moreover the man Moses was exceedingly great in the land of Egypt, in the sight of Pharaoh's servants and of the people.

"And Moses said, Thus says the Lord, About midnight I will go out into the midst of Egypt; and all the first-born in the land [the pride, hope and joy] of Egypt shall die, from the first-born of Pharaoh who sits on his throne, even to the first-born of the maid-servant who is behind the hand mill; and all the first-born of beasts. There shall be a great cry in all the land of Egypt, such as has never been, nor ever shall be again" (11:2-6, Amplified).

God had waited and waited on Pharaoh, and Moses had been patient as he warned Pharaoh of coming judgment. But both God and Moses were to be vindicated. Moses, however, only announced this final judgment, which was entirely from God. The Passover lamb speaks of salvation, and salvation is only of God, although men are used to announce the message.

In the last days the Lord Jesus Christ will be vindicated when He returns to earth. He, in longsuffering, allows mankind now to go against His will, but there will come a time when His omnipotence will be recognized by all. Thus, Christ told the Apostle John, "I am he that liveth, and was dead; and, behold, I am alive for evermore, Amen; and have the keys of hell and of death" (Rev. 1:18).

Under the inspiration of the Holy Spirit, the Apostle John looked ahead to the Second Coming of Christ and wrote: "And out of his mouth goeth a sharp sword, that with it he should smite the nations: and he shall rule them with a rod of iron: and he treadeth the winepress of the fierceness and wrath of Almighty God. And he hath on his vesture and on his thigh a name written, King of Kings, and Lord of Lords" (19:15,16).

These verses refer to that time when the Lord Jesus Christ, with the angels and His saints, will return to earth to bring an end to Gentile world power, which will then be headed up by the Antichrist. After destroying Gentile rule, the Lord Jesus Christ will then establish the kingdom of God on earth.

When God speaks to mankind, it is important that His message not be refused. Hebrews 12:25 says, "See that ye refuse not him that speaketh. For if they escaped not who refused him that spake on earth, much more shall not we escape, if we turn away from him that speaketh from heaven." And verse 29 adds, "For our God is a consuming fire."

As Israel prepared to leave Egypt, God instructed, "Let every man borrow of his neighbour, and every woman of her neighbour, jewels of silver, and jewels of gold" (Ex. 11:2). The word "borrow" does not accurately convey the meaning of the Hebrew word from which it is translated. The Hebrew word is *shaal*, which basically means "to ask."

The Israelites were to ask the Egyptians for the back wages owed them. And because of the respect the Egyptians had learned to have for the Israelites, as well as their fear as a result of the last plague, they gave as they were asked (12:35,36). For many long years the Israelites had toiled as slaves, so what they asked was rightfully theirs. God gave the Israelites favor before the Egyptians, and even this greatly helped Israel to recognize the sovereignty of their God.

In Moses' last words to Pharaoh, he gave God's announcement of a coming plague that would destroy all the firstborn of Egypt (11:4,5). God warned, "There shall be a great cry throughout all the land of Egypt, such as there was none like it, nor shall be like it any more" (v. 6).

God further explained, "But against any of the Israelites either man or beast, not a dog shall bark—to show you how the Lord distinguishes between Egypt and Israel" (v. 7, Berkeley). This is striking proof that every creature is ultimately under the control of the Creator. Imagine the weeping and horror that would sweep across the land on that night, and yet with all of this commotion, a dog would not so much as bark against any of the Israelites.

God's purpose in controlling the dogs was clearly stated: "To show you how the Lord distinguishes between Egypt and Israel" (v. 7, Berkeley). The dogs' remaining quiet while about three million Israelites hustled here and there could only be explained, even by the Egyptians, as a miracle of God. This would cause them to see that God was truly at work.

The ability God had to control the dogs at this time is a reminder of how He later shut the mouths of the lions when Daniel was thrown into their den. Early the next morning, the king hurried to the den and found Daniel safe. The king asked, "O Daniel, servant of the living God, is thy God, whom thou servest continually, able to deliver thee from the lions?" (Dan. 6:20). Daniel replied, "My God hath sent his angel, and hath shut the lions' mouths, that they have not hurt me: forasmuch as before him innocency was found in me; and also before thee, O king, have I done no hurt" (v. 22).

What great power God has, and what a significant contrast there is between the believer and the unbeliever! It should be a tremendous encouragement to every believer to realize that nothing can happen to him unless God allows it.

Having announced the last plague to Pharaoh, Moses said, " 'All these nobles of yours shall come down to me and bow deeply to me, begging of me, Do go out; you and all your followers!' And after that I will go out" (Ex. 11:8, Berkeley). Having said this, Moses "went out from Pharaoh in a great anger" (v. 8).

Moses had endured all he could of Pharaoh's blaspheming God, even at times claiming to confess his sins but evidencing that he was not sincere. The longsuffering of Moses and of God was at an end; the stage was completely set for Israel's emancipation. The Lord told Moses, "Pharaoh will not listen to you, so that My mighty works may multiply in the land of Egypt" (v. 9, Berkeley). Exodus 11 concludes by saying, "Moses and Aaron did all these wonders in the presence of Pharaoh; but the Lord encouraged Pharaoh in his own way and he did not allow the Israelites to leave his country" (v. 10, Berkeley).

A New Beginning

Before detailed instructions were given to Moses concerning Israel's preparation for the Passover, God said to Moses and Aaron, "To you let this month be the first, the month with which your year begins" (Ex. 12:2, Berkeley). In a real sense, this was the beginning of Israel as a nation.

After giving the Israelites detailed instructions for preparing and eating the Passover lamb, God said, "You shall eat it thus: [as fully prepared for a journey] your loins girded, your shoes on your feet, and your staff in your hand; and you shall eat it in haste. It is the Lord's passover" (v. 11, Amplified). As we have said, this haste of the Israelites would have caused much commotion, but not even a dog barked at them.

God told the Israelites, "I will pass through the land of Egypt this night, and will smite all the first-born in the land of Egypt, both man and beast; and against all the gods of Egypt I will execute judgments [proving their helplessness]. I am the Lord" (v. 12, Amplified).

In contrast to the judgment He would bring on the Egyptians, God promised the Israelites, "The blood shall be for a token or sign to you upon [the doorposts of] the houses where you are, [that] when I see the blood, I will pass over you, and no plague shall be upon you to destroy you, when I smite the land of Egypt" (v. 13, Amplified). The blood was the provision for Israel's escape from God's final judgment on Egypt.

Referring to this time and to the leadership that Moses exercised, Hebrews 11:28 says, "Through faith he kept the passover, and the sprinkling of blood, lest he that destroyed the firstborn should touch them."

The significant element in protecting the Israelites was the blood. Some might wonder, Why blood? The Bible emphasizes the importance of blood when it says, "The life of the flesh is in the blood: and I have given it to you upon the altar to make an atonement for your souls: for it is the blood that maketh an atonement for the soul" (Lev. 17:11).

Hebrews 9:22 says, "And almost all things are by the law purged with blood; and without shedding of blood is no remission [forgiveness]." The only way of salvation has been purchased for us by the shed blood of the Lord Jesus Christ. Colossians 1:14 says, "In whom we have redemption through his blood, even the forgiveness of sins."

The Israelites were not able to escape the judgment of the slaying of the firstborn on their own merits but only on the merits of the blood which they applied to the doorposts. It would have been futile for any Israelite to have reasoned that some other action would be acceptable to God. No matter how reasonable some other method might have seemed, nothing was acceptable except the application of the shed blood. So, too, many today think there are several ways of salvation and that sincerity is all that is necessary. But no matter how reasonable this seems, no one will be saved from condemnation unless he applies the shed blood of Christ by believing in Him as personal Saviour.

Israel was not able to escape the Passover judgment just because the people had been chosen by God to be the nation through whom He wanted to specifically work. Although the nation as such was spared, the only way an individual could escape judgment was to exercise personal faith in what God said should be done and to act on that faith.

God's plan of salvation is the same for all people, and all the Old Testament sacrifices of Israel looked forward to the time when Christ would shed His blood for the sins of the whole world. The Bible says, "He is the propitiation for our sins: and not for our's only, but also for the sins of the whole world" (I John 2:2).

No one can buy his way to heaven, as explained in I Peter 1:18,19: "You were not redeemed with perishable things like silver or gold from your futile way of life inherited from your forefathers, but with precious blood, as of a lamb unblemished and spotless, the blood of Christ" (NASB). And as we have pointed out, Hebrews 9:22 reveals that forgiveness is impossible without the shedding of blood.

To those who place their faith in the shed blood of Christ to take away sin, John 6:37 promises, "Him that cometh to me I will in no wise cast out." John 3:18 says, "He that believeth on him is not condemned: but he that believeth not is condemned already, because he hath not believed in the name of the only begotten Son of God." But notice the wonderful promise of Christ recorded in John 5:24: "I say unto you, He that heareth my word, and believeth on him that sent me, hath everlasting life, and shall not come into condemnation; but is passed from death unto life."

After God had finished his instructions to the Israelites concerning the Passover, the Bible says, "The people bowed the head and worshipped. And the children of Israel went away, and did as the Lord had commanded Moses and Aaron, so did they" (Ex. 12:27,28).

The plague came precisely as God said it would: "At midnight the Lord slew every first-born in the land of Egypt, from the first-born of Pharaoh who sat on his throne to the first-born of the prisoner in the dungeon, and all the first-born of the livestock. Pharaoh rose up in the night, he, all his servants, and all the Egyptians; and there was a great cry in Egypt, for there was not a house where there was not one dead" (vv. 29,30, Amplified).

After some of the previous plagues Pharaoh had feigned repentance but had not been willing to let the Israelites leave Egypt. In this case, however, "he called for Moses and Aaron by night, and said, Rise up, get out from among my people, both you and the Israelites; and go, serve the Lord, as you said. Also take your flocks and your herds, as you have said, and be gone! And [ask your God to] bless me also" (vv. 31,32, Amplified).

This action by Pharaoh was a fulfillment of what God had told Moses earlier: "Now shalt thou see what I will do to Pharaoh: for with a strong hand shall he let them go, and with a strong hand shall he drive them out of his land" (6:1).

At his last meeting with Pharaoh, Moses told him, "All these thy servants shall come down unto me, and bow down themselves unto me, saying, Get thee out, and all the people that follow thee: and after that I will go out" (11:8). This verse was fulfilled precisely as Moses said, for after the firstborn of the Egyptians were killed, "the Egyptians were urgent with the people to depart, that they might send them out of the land in haste; for they said, We are all dead men" (12:33, Amplified).

Earlier, God had promised that the Israelites would not leave Egypt empty-handed. He had instructed the Israelites, "Let every man solicit and ask of his neighbor, and every woman of her neighbor, jewels of silver and jewels of gold" (11:2, Amplified). The people did exactly what they were told: "The Israelites did according to the word of Moses; and they [urgently] asked of the Egyptians jewels of silver and of gold, and clothing. The Lord gave the people favor in the sight of the Egyptians, so that they gave them what they asked. And they stripped the Egyptians [of those things]" (12:35,36, Amplified).

No doubt some of the silver and gold which the Israelites requested of the Egyptians was later used in constructing the tabernacle. Perhaps some was even kept and later became part of the temple. Clothing was certainly necessary because the Israelites were headed for the wilderness and did not know how their needs would be taken care of.

Referring to God's deliverance of Israel from Egypt, the psalmist later wrote: "He brought them forth also with silver and gold: and there was not one feeble person among their tribes. Egypt was glad when they departed: for the fear of them fell upon them" (Ps. 105:37,38).

Israel's Indirect Route

When Israel fled Egypt, they could have gone from northern Egypt, where they lived, directly to the land of Canaan. This direct route would have taken only a matter of days. But God knew it was not best for them to go that way because of the enemies they would encounter. The Bible says, "When Pharaoh had allowed the people to go, God did not lead them by way of the Philistines' land, although that was a shorter route; for God considered that, on tasting war, the people might feel regret and go back to Egypt. So God detoured the people toward the desert by the Red Sea. In martial order the Israelites went up from the land of Egypt" (Ex. 13:17,18, Berkeley).

God knew that the tests of faith that the Israelites would face on a direct route to Canaan would be too severe for them, so He led them another way. God also knows the amount of testing that we are able to endure, and I Corinthians 10:13 assures believers, "No temptation has overtaken you but such as is common to man; and God is faithful, who will not allow you to be tempted beyond what you are able; but with the temptation will provide the way of escape also, that you may be able to endure it" (NASB).

There was another reason, however, why God did not take the Israelites on a direct route to Canaan. This reason had to do with Pharaoh. In telling Moses where to camp, the Lord said, "For Pharaoh will say of the Israelites, They are entangled in the land; the wilderness has shut them in. I will harden (make stubborn, strong) Pharaoh's heart, that he will pursue them, and I will get Me honor and glory over Pharaoh and all his host, and the Egyptians shall know that I am the Lord" (Ex. 14:3,4, Amplified).

God impressed on the mind of every Israelite that their deliverance was totally His undertaking, not theirs. He gave the instructions, and He would protect them as they obeyed His instructions. God was fulfilling what He had promised Moses earlier in Exodus 6:6-8.

God had provided and would continue to provide everything needed by the Israelites to accomplish His will. This was especially seen as God led Israel in the path He had chosen and also protected them from the Egyptians by "the pillar of cloud by day and the pillar of fire by night" (13:22, Amplified). The fire at night enabled the Israelites to see where they were going, whereas the Egyptians could not, and the pillar of cloud by day kept the Israelites hidden from the Egyptians.

It is obvious from these events that when God says He will provide for us, He remains absolutely faithful to His word. This fact is especially seen in His plan of redemption for mankind. Throughout Old Testament times the sacrifices looked forward to the Lamb of God who would come to take away sin. God was faithful to His word, and when John the Baptist saw the Lord Jesus Christ, he said, "Behold, the Lamb of God who takes away the sin of the world!" (John 1:29, NASB). God has provided salvation for all mankind, but each individual must personally trust Christ as Saviour in order to have that salvation applied to his life.

A New Era of Leadership

Moses' reaction to all that took place was especially significant. His faith was being tested to the limit as he sought God's strategy for Israel because, humanly speaking, it involved insurmountable obstacles. The Lord said to Moses, "Tell the Israelites to turn back and encamp before Pihahiroth, between Migdol and the [Red] Sea, before Baal-zephon. You shall encamp opposite it by the sea. For Pharaoh will say of the Israelites, They are entangled in the land; the wilderness has shut them in" (Ex. 14:2,3, Amplified).

Here is the situation Moses faced: On the one side was the impassable mountain range of Baal-zephon; on the other side were vast sand dunes which a traveler could not survive; behind Israel was the pursuing Egyptian army; and in front was the Red Sea.

Humanly speaking, they were trapped and would surely be destroyed. But as Hudson Taylor used to emphasize, if the Devil hems you in on all four sides, you can always look up; you can always talk to God. Moses' previous training in God's school really paid off at this time. Although the Israelites could not accept their situation without murmuring and wavering, Moses was able to remain stable because of his faith in God.

Moses realized the truth stated in the New Testament: "Without me ye can do nothing" (John 15:5). Moses had the same concept that was later expressed by the Apostle Paul: "I can do all things through Him who strengthens me" (Phil. 4:13, NASB).

God knew how Pharaoh would reason after the Israelites were gone. Although Pharaoh refused to recognize Him, God knew what was in his heart and how he would think about a given situation. Knowing that Pharaoh's heart was hardened against Him, God told Moses, "I will harden (make stubborn, strong) Pharaoh's heart, that he will pursue them, and I will get Me honor and glory over Pharaoh and all his host, and the

Egyptians shall know that I am the Lord" (Ex. 14:4, Amplified).

Remember that Pharaoh had first hardened his own heart and that God had endured his rebellion with much longsuffering and mercy. But since Pharaoh refused to turn to God in any way, God further hardened his heart in the position he had taken. And Pharaoh demonstrated how hard his heart was. Although many things had occurred which could only be explained as a direct intervention of God, Pharaoh assumed that the Israelites would get entangled and lose their way in the land. He still failed to see that God was delivering the Israelites.

As the Israelites were hemmed in on all sides, their morale must have been at an all-time low. This was their first real test as a nation, and it had to be fully met in order to establish them for what they would face on their journey to Canaan. All they could see was impending death, *but God*—what significant words—*but God* was working in their behalf.

Israel's Spiritual Immaturity

God wanted to teach the Israelites some valuable lessons about trusting in Him, and their situation provided the key opportunity. They could not go in any direction; therefore, they were forced to look up to Him. As the Egyptians pursued them, the Israelites revealed their spiritual immaturity, for they complained to Moses, "Did you take us away to die in the desert because there are no graves in Egypt? Why did you treat us this way, to bring us out of Egypt? Did we not tell you in Egypt, 'Leave us alone; let us serve the Egyptians!' Better for us to work for the Egyptians than to die in the desert" (Ex. 14:11,12, Berkeley).

In their state of spiritual immaturity, the Israelites were able to see only what was around them; their attention was not focused on God. Even when they were not focusing attention on themselves, they were looking to man; they were watching to see what Moses would do. When he did not act as they thought he should, they became discouraged and began to complain and fear for their lives. So we see that the Israelites were still only babes in faith. They needed to exercise their faith before they could be considered spiritually mature.

The Israelites' reactions illustrate the principle that before one can progress with God, he must come to a complete end of himself. As long as the Israelites had reason to trust in themselves, they saw no need to depend on God. But when the circumstances seemed hopeless, thereby bringing them to the end of themselves, they were eventually forced to turn their eyes to God. Then progress was made in their spiritual lives.

This was a counterpart to the New Testament truth that we must die to self before we can live to God (John 12:24). We, too, must realize that we have no might or power against the Enemy; therefore, we need to depend on God. Sometimes God hems us in to teach us to fix our eyes completely on Him.

Although the Israelites were wavering in their faith, Moses' faith remained solid because it was in God, not in others or in himself. Moses had learned from past experience that God does not make mistakes. Even though Moses did not know how God was going to accomplish His will, he was confident that God had a solution to the problem. Previous experiences had taught him that God often has a plan of victory that is far different from any human plan. Although Moses could not see into the future, he moved forward on the basis of his faith in God.

With such confidence in God, Moses spoke to the people and endeavored to instill the same faith in them. Moses admonished them, "Do not fear! Stand by and see the salvation of the Lord which He will accomplish for you today; for the Egyptians whom you have seen today, you will never see them again forever. The Lord will fight for you while you keep silent" (Ex. 14:13,14, NASB). What a statement of faith! These are key verses concerning the unshakable faith that Moses had in God.

God's man had been well prepared, not only intellectually but also experientially. He knew God, and he appropriated the promises of God. Moses' confidence was completely settled in God so that he was full of faith and was able to make such a positive declaration. God's work in him was accomplished! After that God could use him to train others to exercise faith in God. And this is what happened when Moses encouraged the Israelites to take a stand for God.

Reflect on the contrasts we have seen in Moses' life. At age 40 when Pharaoh discovered that he had killed an Egyptian, Moses fled in fear because his eyes were not fixed on God. Even at age 80 when God called him at the burning bush, Moses still had many misgivings. But Moses finally came to the end of himself when he was rejected by his own people (5:21-23), and he learned to put his trust in God only. From this time onward, Moses' faith grew by leaps and bounds. God never moves ahead until He has all things, including His chosen men, well trained and ready to accomplish His will.

So by faith, Moses issued a statement that day which, to a weak and faithless Israel, seemed sheer fantasy. Exodus 14:13,14 records Moses' words which instructed the people to not fear, to stand still, and to see the salvation of the Lord (although God had not given Moses any direct orders of procedure). Let us consider these three commands in more detail.

The Three Commands

Fear not. Israel was completely hemmed in, and a vicious Egyptian army was on its way, and yet Moses said, "Fear ye not" (Ex. 14:13). This statement revealed that Moses was not trusting in human wisdom but in God's wisdom.

Consider some of the situations in which God's people were told not to fear. Abram (Abraham) won a great victory by rescuing his nephew Lot, but he was in serious danger because of the possibility of the defeated armies reorganizing and coming against him. However, God told him, "Fear not, Abram: I am thy shield, and thy exceeding great reward" (Gen. 15:1).

After Joshua had experienced an overwhelming victory at Jericho, he met failure and defeat at Ai. He was afraid that Israel would not be able to face its enemies again. But God told him how to put away the sin from among them and then said, "Fear not, neither be thou dismayed: take all the people of war with thee, and arise, go up to Ai: see, I have given into thy hand the king of Ai, and his people, and his city, and his land" (Josh. 8:1).

When the Lord appeared to Gideon, who later led a small army against great numbers, he was terrified and feared for his life. However, the Lord said to him, "Peace be unto thee; fear not: thou shalt not die" (Judg. 6:23).

When Solomon, the son of David, was anointed king, he faced awesome responsibilities, which included building the temple of God. God encouraged Solomon through the words of David: "Be strong and of good courage, and do it: fear not, nor be dismayed: for the Lord God, even my God, will be with thee; he will not fail thee, nor forsake thee, until thou hast finished all the work for the service of the house of the Lord" (I Chron. 28:20).

When the Lord Jesus Christ was on earth and His followers were discouraged, He told them, "Fear not, little flock; for it is your Father's good pleasure to give you the kingdom" (Luke 12:32).

Perhaps one of the most familiar and best-loved verses that has encouraged believers down through the ages is Psalm 23:4: "Yea, though I walk through the valley of the shadow of death, I will fear no evil: for thou art with me; thy rod and thy staff they comfort me."

Isaiah summed it up beautifully with these words: "Thou wilt keep him in perfect peace, whose mind is stayed on thee: because he trusteth in thee. Trust ye in the Lord for ever: for in the Lord Jehovah is everlasting strength" (Isa. 26:3,4).

Stand still. Even though the Israelites did not know what to do, it seemed totally unreasonable of Moses to expect them to "stand still" (Ex. 14:13). In essence, this was a military order and was equal to telling them to stand by until they received further orders. In many ways, one of the hardest things believers must do is to wait on God. We are impatient just as the Israelites were, and we want to act before God has revealed His plan and purpose to us.

But there comes a time when all activities must stop and we must simply wait on God for His orders. It is part of our human nature to be restless and fidgety; we think we have to be doing something. We often hear the statement, "Don't just stand there; do something!" Faith, however, raises the attention of the believer to the very throne of God, far above the difficulty involved. Such a believer is able to stand still and wait on the Lord.

Earlier, when Moses had come to the end of himself, God said to him, "Now shalt thou see what I will do to Pharaoh" (6:1). But it was not until Moses stood still and waited on the Lord that God acted in his behalf. Following the account of this time of waiting on the Lord, we read God's promise to accomplish Israel's deliverance by Himself (vv. 6-8).

See the salvation of the Lord. Moses exhorted the Israelites to trust God in the face of impending death and to see Him work in their behalf (14:13). Nothing is gained by restless and anxious efforts. The Israelites could not go anywhere or do anything to help themselves. What an opportunity this was for God to teach them great spiritual lessons! This should remind us of Philippians 4:6,7: "Be anxious for nothing, but in everything by prayer and supplication with thanksgiving let your requests be made known to God. And the peace of God, which surpasses all comprehension, shall guard your hearts and your minds in Christ Jesus" (NASB).

Think of how helpless the Israelites were. Could they dry up the Red Sea? Could they level the mountains? Could they bridge the impassable sand? Could they annihilate the armies of Egypt? All of these things were impossible for them to do, but nothing is impossible with God.

It was not necessarily "great" faith that was needed but simply faith in God. When the disciples of Jesus were not able to cast out a demon, they came to Him and asked why. He answered them, "Because of the littleness of your faith; for truly I say unto you, if you have faith as a mustard seed, you shall say to this mountain, 'Move from here to there,' and it shall move; and nothing shall be impossible to you" (Matt. 17:20, NASB).

Moses had passed the test of handling a seemingly impossible situation with flying colors! He was gloriously vindicated in his faith because God at once intervened with a mighty hand and gave him the direction he needed.

The Lord said to Moses, "Why do you call to Me? Tell the Israelites to move forward. Raise your staff and stretch out your hand over the sea; divide it, so that the Israelites may go right through the sea on dry ground" (Ex. 14:15,16, Berkeley).

Notice that Moses did not have to wait for God's orders. When God told him to move forward, He explained how he should go about it. But what an unusual miracle was about to take place! Never had such a miracle occurred before, and it took faith in God to believe that it could occur at this point. Moses had told the people to stand still and see the salvation of the Lord, and God's instructions were a fulfillment of Moses' challenge. They saw salvation which only the Lord could provide.

The Lord delights in shutting His people in to Himself and then displaying His grace and power in achieving the impossible. Just as God did this for the Israelites, He also wants to do it for us. God works in us and through circumstances to accomplish His distinctive will. We all have our trials, and often they seem to present impossibilities as great as the Israelites faced. But even though the Devil can hem us in on all sides, he cannot prevent us from looking to God and depending on Him to deliver us. We can talk to God about our problem and wait on Him to show us the way of deliverance. The Lord's message to us is that we not fear but that we stand still and see His salvation. As we hold our peace, the Lord fights for us.

Throughout the testings and trials of Israel and through the ten plagues God brought on the Egyptians, we see how He fought for His own people all along. He had worked in their behalf before, and He did not fail them at the Red Sea. What a wonderful God we have!

God's Protection

Having instructed Moses to use his staff to divide the Red Sea, God told him, "And I, behold, I will harden the hearts of the Egyptians, and they shall follow them: and I will get me honour upon Pharaoh, and upon all his host, upon his chariots, and upon his horsemen" (Ex. 14:17). Verse 8 records how the Lord hardened Pharaoh's heart so that he pursued the children of Israel, and verse 17 reveals that He hardened the Egyptians' hearts, causing them to follow the Israelites into the Red Sea.

The hearts of the Egyptians were also hardened because they had refused to turn to God, even though they, too, had been given many opportunities for repentance. Pharaoh and the Egyptians revealed that they were truly "vessels of wrath fitted to destruction" (Rom. 9:22). They were "fitted to destruction" because they continuously rebelled against God and refused to obey or even to recognize Him. They had mocked God by refusing His longsuffering and mercy, and God brought an end to their defiance and constant rebellion.

Although judgment was about to come on the Egyptians, God's protecting hand was on the Israelites. The Bible says, "Then the Angel of God, who had been moving ahead of Israel's camp, withdrew and went behind them—the column of cloud withdrew from the front and stood behind them—and came between the camp of Egypt and the camp of Israel; it was cloud and darkness; it also lit up the night; so they did not get close to each other at night" (Ex. 14:19,20, Berkeley).

The cloud protected the Israelites because it was a cloud of darkness to the Egyptians. At night the pillar of fire made it possible for the Israelites to travel, whereas the Egyptians were unable to do so. Thus, we see God's wonderful mercy in protecting His people.

Moses then did as God instructed him: "Moses then stretched out his hand over the sea and the Lord moved the sea all night by a mighty east wind turning the sea into dry land. The waters were divided and the Israelites went into the midst of the sea on dry ground. To their right and to their left the waters formed a wall for them" (vv. 21,22, Berkeley). What marvelous deliverance the Lord provided for His own! They passed through the place of death and were delivered to life.

This reminds us of Romans 6, which tells how the believer is baptized with Jesus Christ into His death and is raised to newness of life (vv. 3,4). Just as the Israelites had life by passing through the place of death, so the believer is made alive to the Lord after trusting Him as Saviour and being identified with Him in His death (Rom. 6:5; Gal. 2:20).

The Lord had said that He would harden the hearts of Pharaoh and the Egyptians so they would pursue the Israelites, and this is precisely what happened. "In hot pursuit the Egyptians followed them, all the horses, the chariots and the horsemen of Pharaoh into the midst of the sea'' (Ex. 14:23, Berkeley). How presumptuous and rebellious can people be? The dividing of the Red Sea was such an obvious miracle of God, yet this fact did not even slow down the Egyptians. All they could think about was capturing the Israelites, so they followed them through the divided waters of the Red Sea.

But notice how God protected His own people by hindering the Egyptians: "Around 6:00 in the morning the Lord looked upon the Egyptian army from the column of fire and cloud and brought on panic among the Egyptian host; He clogged their chariot wheels and made them move so heavily that the Egyptians said, 'Let us get away from the Israelites, for the Lord is fighting for them against the Egyptians' '' (vv. 24,25, Berkeley). What an acknowledgment! The Egyptians realized that the Lord was fighting for the Israelites against them. Moses had told the Israelites, "The Lord shall fight for you, and ye shall hold your peace" (v. 14).

God was completely vindicated; He said that all people would know that He was truly God. Not only did these two nations understand this fact, but all the world was caused to realize it, as evidenced by the song of praise that followed.

As we consider how the Lord acts in behalf of His own, Psalm 118:5-9 is a significant passage: "I called upon the Lord in distress: the Lord answered me, and set me in a large place. The Lord is on my side; I will not fear: what can man do unto me? The Lord taketh my part with them that help me: therefore shall I see my desire upon them that hate me. It is better to trust in the Lord than to put confidence in man. It is better to trust in the Lord than to put confidence in princes." This is God's Holy Word.

We need also to remember the promise of the Lord recorded in Hebrews 13:5,6: "I will never leave thee, nor forsake thee. So that we may boldly say, The Lord is my helper, and I will not fear what man shall do unto me." When we are on God's side, we have nothing to fear because He will fight the battle for us.

When Israel had safely arrived at the east bank of the Red Sea with the Egyptians pursuing them, God said to Moses,

"Stretch out your hand over the sea and let the waters flow back upon the Egyptians, over their chariots and their horsemen. So Moses stretched out his hand over the sea and at break of day the sea returned to its usual flow, with the Egyptians fleeing against it. The Lord tumbled the Egyptians into the middle of the sea. The waves rolled back and submerged the chariots and their drivers together with the whole army of Pharaoh that had followed them into the sea; not even one of them was left" (Ex. 14:26-28, Berkeley). This was God's stroke of death on the enemies of God and Israel.

This is a reminder of how the power of God will be exercised on unbelievers in the end time when the Lord Jesus Christ returns to earth, as recorded in Revelation 19. At that time the Lord Jesus Christ will be vindicated as He brings justice on His enemies.

Some endeavor to explain away the miracles of the Bible. Those who subscribe to liberal theology have even said that it can be proven that the water in the Red Sea at the place where Israel crossed was only about six inches deep at that time of year. But as is often the case, it takes greater faith to believe what liberal theologians say than to believe what the Bible says. What a miracle it would have been if the entire Egyptian army had drowned in only six inches of water!

Complete Deliverance

The deliverance of Israel was finished. It was a complete deliverance, not just a partial one. God had told the Israelites, "I will bring you out from under the burdens of the Egyptians, and I will rid you out of their bondage, and I will redeem you with a stretched out arm, and with great judgments" (Ex. 6:6). When the waters covered the Egyptian army, the Lord had fulfilled His word to Israel—He completely broke the power of Egypt. Egypt still exists as a nation, but it has never been the world power that it was at the time of Moses.

God's breaking the power of Egypt is an illustration of how Christ broke the power of Satan. Hebrews 2:14,15 says, "Since then the children share in flesh and blood, He Himself likewise also partook of the same, that through death He might render powerless him who had the power of death, that is, the devil; and might deliver those who through fear of death were subject to slavery all their lives" (NASB). Just as Egypt still existed after its power was broken, Satan exists now, even though his power has been broken. Believers need not submit to the temptations of Satan; rather, they are to submit to God and resist Satan (James 4:7).

The Egyptian army was drowned in the Red Sea, "but the Israelites had walked on dry ground in the middle of the sea with the waters for their wall to the right and to the left. So did the Lord save Israel that day from Egypt's dominance, and Israel saw the Egyptians dead on the seashore" (Ex. 14:29,30, Berkeley). At first the Red Sea was an impossible wall, or barrier, to the Israelites, but when it was opened up by God, it became a wall of protection on both sides. What a principle this is for us to recognize! Some of the impossibilities we face are actually what God wants to use in our lives to eventually make us what He wants us to be.

The concluding verse of Exodus 14 says, "When Israel looked upon the mighty work which the Lord had wrought upon Egypt, the people revered the Lord and came to believe in the Lord and in His servant Moses" (v. 31, Berkeley). At last Moses was completely vindicated! God was proven true and all powerful. Israel, as well as Moses, was established in faith. All the Egyptian gods were proven completely impotent and even nonexistent.

Exodus 15 records the song of victory which Moses and the Israelites sang to the Lord. This song may have been written prior to this occasion as Moses, by faith, looked ahead to Israel's complete deliverance.

The first 13 verses express the victory that the Israelites had just experienced and relate so well to God's promised deliverance in Exodus 6:6. The next three verses looked ahead to the future victories that Israel would experience as God continued to fight for them. The news of God's deliverance of Israel spread rapidly to other nations, as indicated by Joshua 2:9-11.

Thus concludes this moving account of scripture revealing how God strengthened His man Moses and used him to deliver Israel from Egypt.